FIRE
YOURSELF

REIGNITE YOUR CAREER
AND LIVE YOUR LIFE
WITH INTENTION

LISA BREZONIK & JOHN RUSCIANO

ISBN 13: 978-0-9971289-2-5

Printed in the United States of America
First Printing: 2016
20 19 18 17 16   5 4 3 2 1

To my parents: for teaching me that every day matters and that everything is possible.

— Lisa Brezonik

To my clients: Thank you for making me a part of your life. Here's to your health, wealth, and joy in life!

— John Rusciano

TABLE OF CONTENTS

AUTHOR'S FOREWORD

The kernel for *Fire Yourself!* came from a conversation with my younger brother, who has enjoyed a successful banking career. Years ago, he was employed by a small regional bank that had been promising him ownership while he worked very hard, and successfully so, at saving and then growing their flagship branch. While the lure of ownership kept him engaged, he also recognized that his hard work might be more richly rewarded elsewhere. He shared with me that it was his practice, every two to five years, to act as if he had been fired and go through all the motions accordingly. The first couple of times he felt compelled to stay put, but over time it accelerated his career, and now he works in a much-expanded role for a national bank.

I thought his insight was brilliant and started sharing it with my clients, especially those whose financial plans would put a full and secure retirement within their grasp in a few short years if they stuck to their plan.

At the same time, I recognized that while this guidance brought great comfort to my clients, some took it as permission to coast! "As long as you keep doing what you're doing, you'll be fine" lured them into complacency. I also found myself concerned about clients who had served the same employer for ten or more years and not once ventured outside it, save taking the occasional headhunter call, to see if something better might be available to them.

Then came the Great Recession. Assets of every kind were reevaluated—"marked to market," as it were—and this tremendous upheaval forced all of us to see almost everything of value in a new light.

Without exception, all of my clients whose careers were affected by this event landed on their feet within six months. At the same time, none of us will soon forget how it made us feel about almost everything . . . especially our finances and our careers.

It became my mission not to let this crisis go to waste and to encourage my clients to manage their careers with the same systematic discipline I helped them apply to managing their finances, as they are so closely correlated. On a snowed-in Saturday morning, I started an outline for a book and immediately thought of my client and friend Lisa Brezonik as an ideal partner for a joint project to convey and combine the lessons learned in our practices. I was very excited when she emailed me back, "I'm listening. What did you have in mind?"

I am so grateful and honored to be working with Lisa, for she shares my sincere objective of producing a concise guide to benefit our clients and anyone else who will subscribe to what has become the *Fire Yourself!* process.

We both hope you will find *Fire Yourself!* helpful and that it will serve as a catalyst to taking action and elevating your career to its highest value.

—*John Rusciano*

When John invited me to join this project, I accepted with the goal of balancing his sobering wake-up call with excitement about what is possible when you define what you want and put your resources toward pursuing it. In his message about working to secure your financial future, I saw the potential to build not just a retirement plan, but also a career and life plan supporting your deepest-held goals and values. If you have fifteen or twenty years left in your career—only fifteen or twenty years—let's make the most of it! Wouldn't you rather go through life driving to the destination of your choice? If you're clear on what you want and need in life, you have a much better shot at finding it.

As we finished the first draft of the manuscript, I realized that I was starting to feel unsettled with where I was in my career and the pursuit of my passions. I wasn't sure what I wanted or what was next, so I started using the *Fire Yourself!* process—without even realizing it. I began asking myself and others about who I am and where I want to be and letting go of my assumptions about what I "had" to be doing. Because I was paying attention to what I wanted, I was in the perfect place to recognize and seize a unique opportunity when it appeared. Now I am in a new role, as the Chief Talent Officer at Salo, a finance, accounting, and HR firm, and it's absolutely the right place for me now. I did the work and asked the tough questions, and I ended up happier and better prepared for the next phase of my life and career.

If you take nothing else from this book, I want you to remember that through this entire life, you're never done—done learning, growing, and shaping the life you want. Your wants and needs are always evolving, and it's crucial to keep your values and goals constantly in view. I hope that all of you find this process to be an empowering and clarifying tool for achieving your dreams. You never know what's next!

—*Lisa Brezonik*

INTRODUCTION

There is nothing permanent except change.
—*Heraclitus, Greek philosopher, 540–475 BC*

For at least 2,500 years, humans have recognized that change is a constant. And for nearly as long, we have also recognized that it is our response to change that determines our success.

In our work—John as a financial planner and Lisa as an executive coach and organizational consultant—we strive to help our clients respond to change. And in the best cases, we help them prepare for change as well as initiate change for themselves.

Much of John's work revolves around retirement planning, and the biggest input to that planning is the ability of the client to not only make money but also systematically save it and keep it saved over long periods of time. Lisa helps her clients discern what they want and realize they will have to change their behavior in order to achieve it, and then she coaches them through those changes.

We both help people compare their hopes and dreams with the realities of today's work environment to see where they do and don't match up. We know that a solid career or business leads to a stable income, which reduces the chance that a client's short-term challenges will interfere with their long-term planning. As such, it has always been a part of our service to assist and encourage our clients as they establish, sustain, and grow their careers and mindfully plan for their financial future so they can achieve everything they want in their lives.

We both work with very successful people. However, some have been more successful than others at managing change. Most have embraced it, but some have been blindsided by disruptions to their careers, their plans for retirement, and their hopes and dreams. Heraclitus had it right about the permanency of change. But changes today are coming faster and from every direction— and so are new opportunities. Everyone is advised to be on the lookout for change, to prepare for it, and even to take advantage of it!

The career path that once seemed so predictable can suffer a detour or even vanish in an instant. Exciting new opportunities can open up at exactly the wrong moment. The retirement plan that was supposed to be comfortable can be threatened over-night. And though some changes are unpredictable, many are very predictable indeed, if not in specifics, at least in their gener-al characteristics. The clues have always been there, though not always obvious.

In both financial and career planning, some people face sig-nificant challenges in setting and reaching their goals. Retirement may arrive before they are prepared for it—financially or other-wise. The new life chapter they hoped for is out of reach. Their sense of career security is eroding. They may realize they are do-ing work that doesn't feed their souls. And these challenges can occur as easily at age thirty-five as they can at age fifty-five.

But there are others, as well: clients who have made the choice to take control of their careers. They have responded to econom-ic challenges by saving more, reducing debt, living within their means, and valuing the nonmonetary blessings in their lives. They have faced career detours calmly and been prepared to take ad-vantage of new paths as they appeared.

The things we learned from working with both types of clients led us to write *Fire Yourself!* In this concise guidebook for creating financial stability through a meaningful career, we provide you with ways to gain more control over how you think about, plan for, and ultimately achieve your financial, career, and life goals. In short, *Fire Yourself!* will help you figure out what you want and how to get it.

It is also a wake-up call for those who may be coasting, knowingly or not, toward retirement. Our aim is to help you to make the most of the current phase of your career and to take steps to ensure that your financial situation and the career that drives it will allow you to successfully retire in every sense of the word—and stay retired if you so choose.

Ours is a positive message! We want you to enjoy your life and career, especially in the last leg. We want to equip you to realize all of your hopes and dreams and have the personal life, work life, and retirement life that you really want.

Getting there will require some work on your part; there's no magic bullet here. We will ask you to think differently about your future and then take action to create that future and to be more proactive, more mindful, and more successful in planning and creating your career and financial stability.

We know from experience that when clients take control, they can have the lives they really want. Most people want to be successful, but to be attainable, that success must be clearly articulated and well planned. And that is sometimes the most difficult part.

Wherever you are in your work life—just starting out, well established, job hunting, at a plateau, or approaching retirement—this book is for you. We will show you how you can create the life you want, one of purpose and meaning. We want to help you enjoy the journey of work as well, so in addition to planning for the future, we'll address the realities of working, earning, and advancing in today's world. And to know where you are, you have to know how you got here.

Welcome to the first steps in creating the future you desire. Why wait for something to happen? Those who are fully engaged in planning and managing their own careers are more successful and more fulfilled. Are you?

CHAPTER 1

FIRE YOURSELF!

"If you don't like change,
you'll like irrelevancy even less."
—*General Eric K. Shinseki, former Army Chief of Staff*

If there is one overriding truth, it is this: change is inevitable.

Successful change is anything but. Success requires taking control of your own affairs and figuring out what is best for you. It requires a strategy.

This book is for everyone in the workplace, not just those who have already experienced the pain of losing a job or the frustration of ending up in an unfulfilling position. It's for those who realize that they can take responsibility for their careers, their financial futures, and their lives.

Now, some people will choose to keep their heads down and hope for the best. We wish them the best, but we know it's a terribly risky strategy.

But if you're ready to grab the reins of your life and make the changes needed to thrive in this brave new world, let's get to it.

The core of our process is this: If you were fired today, what are the steps—all the steps—you would take today to replace your job? If that meant you could be doing exactly what you want to be doing at work and in your life, what would it take?

Avoiding the traps lurking between you and your goals requires two significant shifts: first in your thinking and then in your actions. So we recommend this simple strategy for making both shifts:

Fire Yourself!

Simple. But not easy.

The *Fire Yourself!* process is about focusing on the possible, not necessarily what is happening or about to happen. It's a chance to dig into your career toolbox, throw out the rusty ones, clean up others, and add the tools you'll need for the future.

If you're currently doing fine, it's possible you could be doing even better. If you are in a situation where change is threatening your future, *Fire Yourself!* shows you how to take control and get back on track . . . the track you really want to be on.

One important safety tip: When we say *"Fire yourself!"* we don't mean that you should literally quit your job. But just for the moment, let's consider the worst-case scenario. If you'd just been fired, what would you do?

Once the unthinkable has happened, your options become limited. But by firing yourself mentally, starting the process before it actually happens, you can examine all of the relevant factors without the economic and emotional pressure of needing to replace income.

Fire Yourself! is a way of thinking and acting strategically to ensure that you have the career and financial future that you really want, whether you've recently lost a job or are wondering how to get from here to your dream career. It's a way of taking control of your future by examining yourself, your career, and your hopes and dreams. And then choosing actions that will get you where you really want to be.

Here's something else to keep in mind: employee development is driven by employees, not managers or companies. Organizations look to develop people they believe in. Who do they believe in? Motivated, ambitious, smart people who have demonstrated the ability to succeed and to continually evolve in their own subject matter expertise or in their contribution to the company's growth and strategy.

Most companies that are growing and managing well for their future set time aside each year to discuss their high-potential employees (those with the ability to take on more responsibilities in the future) and succession planning. The leaders of the organization make decisions about how and who to develop—which employees they will tap to take the company into the future. People are watching and paying attention to your performance even if you don't think they are. Sliding under the radar is not a good thing.

Taking strategic control of your career means asking yourself some very important questions:

- Do I really enjoy my current job? If so, what do I love about it?
- Do I feel valued? Am I making the kind of contribution I want to make?
- If things changed at work tomorrow, would I look for the same job I have now somewhere else? Or would I search for something different?
- What additional skills or experience do I need, for this role or a new one?
- How do what I know and what I need fit into the current world?
- Who do I need to be talking to?
- How do I need to "show up"?
- Where could I be of the most value?
- What could I do that would feed my soul?
- What am I really worth in today's market? What can I do to increase that?

Fire Yourself! lays out a strategy for getting control over your own career and retirement. There is much in today's world that is not in our control. Doesn't it make sense to take control of everything you can? That includes how you think about yourself, your job, your finances, and your future. It also includes identifying potential opportunities and challenges, taking action when possible, and doing it now, not when you've run out of options. As one of those motivated, ambitious, smart people, you owe it to yourself to participate in the evolution of your own growth and strategy as well as your company's.

LISA SIDEBAR

I am often hired by executives to use this exact philosophy to coach people on their team. Leaders want fresh, skilled, empowered employees. That is what the *Fire Yourself!* process is all about. If you can figure out how you can best contribute to an organization in a way that makes both you and your organization successful, you will be just that—successful.

It's not rocket science, but too many people don't do the work required. They get lazy, and that laziness shows in their contribution . . . or lack thereof.

Anthony's Story

A couple years ago, John was working with Anthony, a successful, fifty-something executive whose employer paid him well and had helped him amass a substantial amount of wealth in the twenty-plus years of his tenure there. In light of how long Anthony had worked for one employer and how many more years he hoped to work, to pay for his kids' college educations and complete the funding of his retirement, John decided to share with him the *Fire*

Yourself! concept.

Anthony replied that he enjoyed working for his company, liked the culture there, and felt there was still a substantial opportunity to acquire more stock in the company in the same manner he had in the past.

He heard the message, but it didn't resonate with him at that moment.

A few months later, the company offered voluntary separation packages to all of its employees and outlined management changes that left Anthony thinking the prudent move would be to grab one of the packages for himself.

When he met with John to evaluate the options available to him, he recalled our *Fire Yourself!* conversation and its emphasis on being proactive, assessing the market for his talents and experience even if he had no plans to leave his employer.

Given the short deadline for opting into voluntary separation, Anthony felt ill-prepared to enter the job market. As a result, and despite the many months of income his separation package represented, he still felt pressured—"behind the eight ball"—about getting back into the job market and securing a replacement position.

Ironically, when he updated his long-neglected LinkedIn profile with his last role at his now past employer, the system sent out a "Congratulate Anthony, who has a new job" message, confusing all of his contacts at the very time he wanted them to be on the lookout for opportunities for him!

He had no idea where to set his compensation expectations, very little online presence, a stagnant network of contacts, and little sense of the job market at the VP/general manager level, and he hadn't interviewed for a job in years.

He admitted that he should have listened to John back then, for had he done so, he would have been substantially more confident and prepared.

But even though it was late, it wasn't too late to engage in the *Fire Yourself!* process. As it turned out, Anthony soon found a position that he was excited about, with substantial potential to provide even more for himself and his family.

GET UNCOMFORTABLE

Change requires courage and a willingness to be uncomfortable. Humans naturally resist and fear change; we like things to stay the same. But as we've seen, they don't stay the same. Ever.

Growth and comfort cannot coexist. You can't learn anything if you never get out of your comfort zone.

But if you have the courage to be uncomfortable—systematically, periodically, and deliberately—opportunities will present themselves left and right. You can have the career you want, the financial wealth you want, the retirement you want, and the life you want.

The best strategy is to anticipate change, to choose to make significant changes before you have to. That means valuing learning over knowing and constantly seeking to add to your value, your choices, your abilities, and your possibilities. However, while it's clearly the best long-term strategy, anticipation requires a willingness to be uncomfortable.

LISA SIDEBAR

Sometimes being good at your job and having experience is not enough. Sometimes, career survival is dumb luck.

A large medical device manufacturer decided to cut costs by letting 10 percent of the people go in one division. But the criteria was not productivity, or tenure, or work ethic; it was attachment to an ongoing project. If you weren't involved with a project, or were working on a project that was coming to an end, you were out.

The result was the loss of many senior people, people that the company had invested lots of time and money to develop. Those people might have thought that investment would shield them from layoffs; perhaps they even became complacent.

In the end, even though you may do all the right things, events are not always within your control. You have to be ever-vigilant, ever-prepared for random, unplanned career disruptions . . . even if that's uncomfortable.

When we introduce the *Fire Yourself!* concept, we often get the following response: "Yeah, this makes total sense. But what if my employer finds out?"

Our answer is, "Don't kid yourself!" Know that the people "upstairs" are talking about you every month, every quarter, and every year. They are evaluating, quantifying, and ranking your value to the organization, whether you are aware of it or not.

Why shouldn't you be doing the same thing? Moreover, if you are a valuable asset, they already assume that you are always keeping your options open and that you receive periodic calls from recruiters and competitors.

JOHN SIDEBAR

When I began working with Davis, he was president of four companies that formed a closely held, family-owned enterprise. As a result of the economic downturn and other factors outside of Davis' control, the family ownership group abruptly installed a new management team. Now fifty years old, Davis found himself on the outside of a company he'd thought he had a shot at owning someday. As a result, he had never considered what the job market was like or what other options might be available to him.

What Davis did next is a story I have shared with many clients and friends, because it is such a clear example of what to do.

Davis turned finding a job into a full-time job: up early every morning, phoning, e-mailing, and networking until he found a new job.

But that's not the real lesson here . . .

The real lesson is that the new job was there all the while. Had Davis fired *himself*, he would have found it proactively and started his new career sooner, and perhaps with less effort. As it was, he was lucky that the job was still available after he was fired.

Now CFO of a major regional company with millions in revenue and hundreds of employees, Davis has never made more money, had more potential to build wealth for his family and his future, or most importantly, enjoyed his work more than he does now.

And that leads us to the message behind all of our work:
Don't be done.
Only you can decide who you are, what you value, and what

path you want your life to take. Don't be done figuring out who you are and where you're going. You'll almost certainly face setbacks and detours on the path, but you don't have to fear them. With *Fire Yourself!*, you are in control.

This book gives you the questions you must ask of yourself, over and over, to make sure that you're living the life that you want. Change is constant. We'll walk you through some tough questions, but you'll soon find that the answers come easier once you've set yourself deliberately on the path to what you really want to achieve in your life, your career, and your retirement.

Don't be done chasing it!

WHY FIRE YOURSELF?

---

*The trouble with the future is that it usually
arrives before we're ready for it.*
—*Arnold H. Glasow*

Firing yourself has never been so important as it is today. Just a quick glance at the headlines—or at the empty offices in even stable companies—proves that change is guaranteed. And nothing illustrates Arnold Glasow's statement so clearly as the rise of the Internet.

There is no part of today's world that has not changed—and won't continue to change—because of the global access to information, speed of information transfer, and ability to bridge physical distance the Internet provides. Information is now instantly available everywhere at once. Industries, companies, and employment are all being defined and redefined. Whether it's the creation of a new industry, product, or service or rapid capitalization on a new opportunity, today's world is being shaped by what economist Joseph Schumpeter called "creative destruction."

SIDEBAR

The development of personal computers, standardized protocol, hypertext, and the World Wide Web led to a breathtaking increase in both users and utilization. Consider: during the late 1990s, the mean annual growth in the number of Internet users was estimated at between 20 and 50 percent, while traffic on the public Internet grew by 100 percent per year. In 1995 there were 16 million Internet users; today that number is nearly 3 billion.

New enterprises appear overnight, throwing venerable incumbents into chaos. Amazon was at first a threat only to bookstores, but it quickly expanded to threaten retailers in music, clothing, hardware, toys . . . you name it, Amazon probably sells it. E-commerce has disrupted everything from publishing to banking. When's the last time you used a paper map? A phone book? A travel agent? Connectivity has transformed supply chains, increased productivity, and reduced costs to the degree that firms such as Wal-Mart have crushed national names such as Sears and tiny local retailers alike. Even yard sales are not immune; why haul everything out to the driveway and sell to the neighbors when you can list it on eBay and sell to the world?

JOHN SIDEBAR

I was looking for a handyman, and where I might once have used the Yellow Pages or asked around for names, I instead subscribed to Angie's List. I read the reviews, both good and bad, and found someone who worked out very well.

In today's marketplace, it's easy to find great people . . . as well as not-so-great people. Online reviewers—professional and amateur alike—rate companies and name names in posts that stick around for years, whether or not their opinions are accurate. Your performance is instantly rated and instantly public. And in business, those that get bad reviews can't survive for long.

In some ways, this is nothing new. Companies have been put out of business by innovative competitors for as long as there have been companies. The Pony Express, a remarkably successful enterprise, was shuttered after only eighteen months by the telegraph and railroad. What is new is the speed at which information is gathered, shared, and exploited and how the most durable companies can be brought to their knees with breathtaking velocity.

JOHN SIDEBAR

The Encyclopædia Britannica was the gold standard in information for nearly two hundred years. Their product was expensive, but parents aspired to acquire the set for their kids. Even today, it enjoys tremendous brand recognition. But they went from massive profits to losses in a few short years, due to the advent of digital multimedia such as Microsoft's Encarta and free online competitors such as Wikipedia. Today, the Encyclopædia Britannica is no longer available in book form.

For industries and companies, this new environment creates winners and losers. The same holds true for individuals, as well. The free flow of information has compressed the business cycle of entire industries, the business cycle of the companies that occupy those industries, and as a result, the careers that depend on them.

Jobs are being eliminated, altered, and outsourced. Virtually every job in the marketplace has new and continually changing requirements for employees. Entire categories of jobs that were previously considered "safe" are now gone or radically altered. If you are a manager of an inside function such as a call center, HR, or accounting, you may already have seen those functions—and perhaps even your own job—outsourced. Even jobs that seemed impossible to outsource have been affected. For example, the fact that face-to-face meetings can now be accomplished online via Skype or GoToMeeting has reduced demand for meeting planners, hotel and airline personnel, and even taxi drivers.

This is why the *Fire Yourself!* process has never been more important. The only way you can hope to manage the immense changes is to take charge of your career, your retirement, and your future.

FACING THE FACTS
A recent Oxford University study predicts that 47 percent of the occupational categories into which work is customarily sorted are at high risk of being automated within the next two decades—including many white-collar jobs. Where do you hope to be in that time period? Is that plan based on an assumption that the marketplace—in this time of unprecedented change—will remain the same?

The hard truth is that once the talent and resources possessed by a company are no longer employed to their highest and best use, they tend to gravitate to another company or industry. Sometimes individuals make that choice; other times, that choice is made for them. Those who are unprepared to make that move are left with slim pickings indeed.

Careers are now inexorably tied to our role in a global economic "food chain." Events across the globe have an impact on what we do and how we do it. Innovations fundamentally change the nature of our work. Changing requirements within our organizations can force us to learn new skills, adapt to the new reality, or even begin a new job search.

The facts aren't all bad, though. LinkedIn, online job applications, and prospective employer research have all transformed how employers recruit and hire their workforces. Technology has removed inefficiencies from the system and added transparency, creating both opportunities and challenges, and the impact of this effect is—or soon will be—individualized. If you're looking for a job, it's much easier today to find out who's hiring for what. At the same time, the candidate pool is much larger. In effect, you're competing with everybody.

The same is true for employers. They have access to many more potential hires but can be overwhelmed by the number of applications they receive. Conversely, they are at risk of head-hunters poaching their employees on a daily basis.

LISA SIDEBAR

When organizations are interviewing for new blood—especially leaders—they interview for the skill of managing change and adaptability. It is no longer a "nice to have" competency. Being able to navigate into the future is now a requirement for most organizations.

I often am asked to help work with teams: new teams, old teams, self-diagnosed "dysfunctional" teams, inexperienced teams, and so on. When I ask what is going on with the team, why they need help, the answer is always change.

The fact that most companies now train their leaders to deal with change is itself a change. Change management has become a required discipline. Preparing yourself to face it makes you a more desirable resource in the work world as well.

The one thing you can be assured of is that change is here to stay. And you'd better get comfortable—and skillful—at dealing with it.

That means taking action. You have to be willing to change. Hockey great Wayne Gretzky once said, "I skate to where the puck is going to be, not where it has been." You have to move in the direction of where you will be and want to be, not where you've been.

Especially when it comes to planning your career and retirement. And the *Fire Yourself!* process will help you do just that.

THE TRAPS

A trap is only a trap if you don't know
about it. If you know about it, it's a challenge.
—*China Miéville*

The changing nature of our world—in both personal lives and work lives—has created significant traps for people planning for their careers and retirement. The new realities of the work world require new thinking and new actions. As we work with our clients to build strong careers and financial stability, we encounter four significant traps that people fall into again and again.

TRAP #1: IT CAN'T HAPPEN TO ME

Often we meet clients who have a false sense of security in their careers. This may be because they've always enjoyed success in a career on a steady rise in responsibilities, prestige, and income.

Sharon's Story

It was a wonderful career, steadily rising through the ranks of a large—and very successful—retail organization. There had always been an implied contract: if Sharon worked hard and met each new challenge, the company would always have a place for her. And for seventeen years, that implied contract had served Sharon very well.

Her latest position had been in an important region, and as always, she excelled. As a result, Sharon was tapped to work on a special project at the home office.

The home office! Over the years, Sharon had seen people brought in to the home office and from there rise to the most senior levels of the company. This was the biggest opportunity yet. She would further her reputation and visibility at the highest levels of the organization. She would be at the nerve center of the organization, at the levels where big decisions were made. And Sharon would be at—or at least closer to—the head table.

So with a mixture of excitement and apprehension, Sharon packed up and moved across the country. She looked forward to the challenge of the special project, trusting that when it ended, the implied contract would present a new and even more prestigious position. Her future was secure.

Now fifty-nine, Sharon planned to work for the company until retiring at sixty-five. She envisioned the last six years of her career as much the same as the rest: success, advancement, and financial security. She had started as an HR specialist; she now dared to see herself becoming VP of HR for the entire company.

But that's not how it worked out . . .

When the special project ended, Sharon was called to a meeting with her boss. She had been to many meetings like this before: recognition for her supreme efforts, adulation for the success of the project, and a discussion of her next opportunity.

The meeting that awaited her was much different. In addition to her boss, Sharon was surprised to see an HR colleague, one who specialized in outplacement. Her boss said that he appreciated the job Sharon had done with the special project, but he was very sorry; there was no further position available for her. He thanked her for her years of service, and the HR specialist started to go over the details of her separation package.

Sharon barely heard a word of it. This was so far away from anything she had even imagined that she could barely breathe. When asked if she had any questions, Sharon could only murmur, "No." And with that, the meeting—and her seventeen-year career with that company—were over.

She didn't know how long she sat in her car, unable to leave the home office parking lot. Sharon felt victimized by the company . . . the company to which she had given everything! What had she done wrong? She had worked hard, followed the rules, and succeeded at every turn, only to be betrayed at the pinnacle of her career. Slowly, the realization dawned on Sharon: the implied contract was just that—implied. There was never a promise, never even an understanding that she would be able to stay until retirement.

Far from friends and family, still a stranger in a city that was dominated by the company that had discarded her, Sharon was in a state of shock. Unemployed for the first time in her career, she now doubted everything. She couldn't understand what had happened, how it had gone so very wrong, how they could treat her this way, how this could happen to her.

And she had no idea what to do next.

The reality of today's working world is that even well-educated, previously successful professionals are not immune from disruption. New leadership, shifting budget priorities, new technology, mergers and acquisitions, qualified workers willing to do the same job for less money—all can devalue once-durable experience and skills and derail a career.

People fall into Trap #1 because they believe that they (and their company) are immune to workplace disruptions or think that because they have survived past disruptions they will survive future disruptions as well. But continuous change puts everything—every job, every career, every individual—at risk; the next disruption may have no similarities to the last one. Market forces that used to effect slow, incremental change—the type that you could have seen coming and prepared for—are now forcing discontinuous, comprehensive change faster than ever.

As a result, the things we count on—our skills, our experience, our knowledge—may no longer give us traction in our current position or company. And then what?

JOHN SIDEBAR

In my financial planning practice, we call this "survivor bias." The longer we survive having not planned properly (e.g., not buying life insurance), the longer we think we can wait before planning or taking proactive steps. But the fact that any given risk hasn't become reality makes it no less real a risk.

TRAP #2: I KNOW WHAT I'M WORTH

Most people have a clear idea of what they are worth. And most of them are wrong.

When assessing our value, we often look at past performance: what we've been paid, our years of experience, and our acquired knowledge and skills.

When someone assigns a value to any asset—its "book value"—they may use a range of assumptions or formulas, including what was paid for the asset, what the current owner would accept in a theoretical sale, or its value based on an assumed rate of growth calculated from the time the asset was acquired.

In contrast, the phrase "mark to market" refers to valuing an asset based on its current value in its respective marketplace today, even (or especially) if the market for that asset is temporarily depressed. In this way, marking an asset to market is also a sort of stress test to assess the owner's ability to weather a wider range of market conditions.

JOHN SIDEBAR

The term "mark to market" has been around as long as I can remember, but it gained prominence during the financial crisis of 2008–2009. I use the term to help my clients assess the value of their skills and experience to the marketplace in which they are "sold."

One example I often use that resonates with my clients is this: we all think we know what our house is worth . . . until we try to sell it. Only then do we know what it's truly worth. Moreover, entering the selling process usually entails a conversation with a real estate professional in which we learn the changes we need to make to our home to make it more valuable and marketable. This analogy applies to any asset . . . especially our careers.

The "book value" of a career is often deemed to be what it currently pays. Essentially, it means valuing our current package of skills and experience with one data point. Marking ourselves to the market—that is, discovering the true market value of our current skills and experience—could yield a value higher or lower than what we are currently being paid, and doing so thus requires more data points. It means putting the asset out there to see what the broader market has to say about our value so that we can act proactively and on a more informed basis.

The Mechanics' Story

In August of 2005, the mechanics union went on strike against Northwest Airlines, rejecting a contract that called for 25 percent wage cuts. Union leadership assumed the mechanics' value to the airline was the same as it had been in past years. But things were different: after 9/11, air travel suffered as economic conditions, fear reduced America's appetite for nonessential air travel, and carriers were reluctant to grow capacity under the weight of heightened security and volatile fuel prices. As a result, the demand for airline workers declined at the same time that mechanics downsized from other airlines were willing to work for lower wages and benefits.

The turmoil and changing economics of the airline industry were readily apparent to most of the world. The industry was experiencing radical transformation, with drastic cost-cutting, extra passenger fees, and the loss of leverage previously held by unions and employees.

But in 2005, the Northwest mechanics didn't see that. Union leadership led them to believe they were worth more to Northwest than they actually were. Instead of individually taking responsibility for their jobs and financial futures, they held out for a contract that was never going to be on the table. Just over a year later, the union settled for 30 percent wage cuts and significantly lower employment levels for their members. Most never returned to work, and those who did took significant pay cuts.

This story is a stark example of a failure to "mark yourself to market"—accurately determining the current value of your experience, skills and knowledge—and failing to take individual responsibility for your economic relevance.

If you only look at book value and ignore market value, you can easily fall into Trap #2. Often this means overvaluing your own worth and then being surprised when your employer sees things very differently. Other times it means undervaluing your worth, which may keep you from discovering other opportunities.

Either way, if there is a gap between your career's "book value" (or perceived value) and its true market value, the market tends to eventually correct this gap.

Roger's Story

As he approached his ten-year anniversary at a large, privately held company, things were going very well for Roger . . . very well indeed. As a department manager, Roger oversaw the activities of fifty-eight people, including four direct reports (three supervisors and one administrative assistant). The department was humming along, and Roger's personal evaluations were always excellent.

He was comfortable in his job, did it well, and had no interest in moving any higher up. He didn't want his boss's VP position. And as for the higher levels of the organization—SVPs, EVPs, and C-levels—well, Roger was more than happy to leave the headaches to them. He understood every nook and cranny of his department and was content to stay right where he was.

One Friday night his phone rang at home. It was one of his supervisors, wondering if Roger knew anything about the company being sold. Roger assured him that if it were true, surely someone would have informed them.

On Monday morning, the news broke: a private equity firm

had bought Roger's company. The new owners talked about the value of their new purchase, how they would be creating more growth, and stressing they had no plans for widespread changes.

For Roger, it seemed like good news. As a shareholder, he would enjoy the benefits of the takeover. As a department manager, he felt the new owners might provide additional investment for the future.

What Roger didn't know was that the new owners viewed the company as overstaffed and inefficient. Within two weeks, it was announced that the company was being streamlined. The many layers of management would be drastically reduced. And one of those layers was department managers.

Roger was given a choice: he could take a severance package (which he considered stingy given his success and years of service), or he could become a supervisor (which he considered a humiliating demotion).

Roger saw himself as a valuable individual with unique skills that made him an asset to the organization. The new owners viewed him as a number, an expense that needed to be cut, a position that added no real value anymore.

In the end, Roger took the severance package, certain that his abilities would quickly land him a similar position within the industry. But it soon became apparent that what had happened to his company was happening all over. Middle managers were an endangered species, and the few positions that were available were being filled by people younger and less experienced than Roger—people who would work for much less money.

If your current job relies on a skill—whether it came via experience, advanced degrees, or a trade school or union—the changing workplace landscape and the market for your skill determine its economic value. And that value can change quickly.

Avoiding this trap requires being willing to continually examine your real worth in the current market, because be sure of this:

someone else is. Customers, senior management, and shareholders are always marking you to market. And if they come to a different conclusion than you do, the results can be catastrophic.

TRAP #3: I HAVE PLENTY OF TIME

Today people are starting significant phases of their lives much later than the previous generation did. They are getting married later; according to the US Census Bureau, the median age of first marriages has risen from twenty-two in 1950 to twenty-nine in 2014. People are starting families well into their thirties and even into their forties.

The current job market and economic environment mean thousands of college graduates find themselves underemployed, moving back home, or both, all of which may delay getting married, starting a family, buying a home, or building a career. This will create a ripple effect on workers of all ages for generations to come.

Instead of following the old career path—work hard, stay in the same field or with the same company, steadily advance, retire at sixty-five—people find their careers taking off later, often with several twists and turns along the way. And yet many still plan on retiring at the same age as previous generations.

Therein lies the trap.

JOHN SIDEBAR

I was nearly thirty years old when my first child was born; in contrast, my father was in his early twenties when I, his first child, arrived. That's typical; we are often at least ten years older than our parents were when they started families and careers. Yet we still hope to retire at the same age. That requires different thinking about our financial planning. We need to be benchmarking our retirement planning more realistically.

In my experience, no matter how well our clients are set up financially, they almost never retire while they have kids in college!

Starting later extends the goals and obligations for which we work well into what traditionally would have been our retirement phase. A forty-year-old having a child today will be almost sixty when the child starts college—which means that retirement savings may take a backseat to contributions to that child's education. It's often mathematically impossible for today's midcareer adults to retire at age sixty-five with the same financial security their parents enjoyed.

There's one other factor at play: the "bionic retirement" of increased life expectancy. Breathtaking advances in health care are extending both the years of our lives and the life in our years. In the future, we will have access to real-time diagnostics, improved drugs and treatments, and even the ability to grow (or 3D print) new organs designed specifically for us.

According to World Bank statistics, in 1960 the average life expectancy in the United States was just under sixty-nine years. Today, it's nearly seventy-nine. What will it be by the time you are ready to retire?

JOHN SIDEBAR

When we assemble a financial plan for a client, retirement is the centerpiece. The goal is to gather the clients' facts and feelings related to wants and needs, lifestyle, cash-flow needs, and time horizon. When a client has a desire to retire early, or even at the "standard" age of sixty-five, we try to help the client understand what happens from there—all the factors that could impact their ability to retire and stay retired.

Retired clients face a litany of risks: from the market, from inflation, from legislation, and not least, from longevity. To assess longevity risk, we don't use average life expectancies. Instead, I like to ask clients about their parents, siblings, aunts, and uncles. Our standard assumption is that clients will live to age ninety-five, but of late I haven't been sure even that is long enough. An average retirement timeframe is already thirty years, let alone any impact future medical developments could have. The point? Planning for thirty years of retirement, even with rather substantial assets, can be a tall order. The risk of outliving one's savings is increasing.

My message is that the retirement goal is not when you plan to exit the workplace. Rather, it is the point when your financial capital can replace your need to utilize your human capital—that is, your labor—if you choose to or have to. Once my clients understand the substantial assets required to fund a long retirement, many of them move their retirement date farther out. We'll talk more about these challenges in chapter 9.

Retiring today at sixty-five may mean ten additional years of retirement. Good news if you have planned your retirement well. Bad news if you haven't.

Because we are starting later and live longer, we have to adjust our planning to ensure that both our careers and our hoped-for retirement are on the right trajectory—and the earlier that planning begins, the better.

TRAP #4: MY CAREER IS A SURE THING

Well-meaning parents have always coached their children to choose "good" careers. Many parents dream of having a child become a doctor or lawyer. Others believe that learning a trade or acquiring a specific skill would mean their child's skills would always be in demand.

But, as we've shown, nothing is immune from the dynamic forces of change. Being a highly skilled blacksmith is not the good career choice it once was. Every trade, every job, every set of skills is subject to change, often without much warning. Even the dream jobs have lost some of their luster. Financially, a medical school graduate is faced with enormous student loan debt and the high cost of malpractice insurance, as well as an erosion of earnings. Law graduates also face enormous debt and liability insurance fees, plus a glutted post-recession market.

Trap #4 is thinking that a career choice is a "sure thing," when in reality every career has the potential to be an endangered species. Making one career choice and considering yourself set for life is mystical thinking.

LISA SIDEBAR

My dad is a retired dentist. To this day, he beams when he talks about his career and his impact. He truly loved his work.

However, if you ask his advice for young people thinking of getting into dentistry today, you may be surprised by his response. He answers:

So you want to be a dentist. Ask yourself why. Is it to make money or have prestige in the community? Not *a good enough reason. Remember: to get there it's a rigorous challenge academically. Only 5 percent of applicants will be accepted into dental school. And it's eight years of college and training with a minimum school debt of $250,000 to $300,000. It's important that you passionately want to make a difference in helping others while doing something that is challenging to you behaviorally, using your optimal strengths and gifts.*

If you pursue it with these qualifiers, then you will reap the aforementioned rewards and lifetime satisfaction.

If you are prepared for one specific job or career, you limit your potential value and your ability to adapt to the shifting marketplace. Instead, you have to think of your knowledge and skills in a wider context. For example:

- A CPA with a degree in finance can do more than prepare tax returns; any position with a financial component may offer opportunities.
- A law degree can be a valuable credential in many fields and organizations.
- An engineering degree might offer value and relevant skills beyond a typical engineering role.

Ann's Story

Ann was a college senior starting to think about how to land a solid job upon graduation. A smart student who relied on her intellect to get her through any door that interested her, she was lucky enough not to have had to work while in college; although it meant she had no practical experience, it did allow her to focus on her studies. She had decided on a major that was very specific to a narrow set of roles in the corporate world.

Determined to find a job in her field, Ann actually turned down her contacts' offers to introduce her into companies with positions that didn't exactly fit her narrow focus. She met several times with Lisa to explore opportunities and ideas for networking and uncovering leads, but she was not willing to look at anything not directly related to the exact job that she wanted. And in the spring, when she still had no leads, she didn't see a need to take an interim role.

After a year of searching, she still didn't like her options. She enrolled in grad school, where she became stronger in her areas of study yet even more narrowly pigeonholed into a field where opportunities for individuals with zero experience were few and far between.

About eighteen months after obtaining her graduate degree, Ann landed a role. It wasn't exactly what she thought she would be doing, but it was time to start earning her own way and seemed like it could lead to an even more interesting position.

In the end, Ann had to compromise. She realized that many of her colleagues had earned tenure by entering the workforce four years earlier than she did. They commanded stronger wages as well as the political know-how that enabled many of them to climb the corporate ladder.

Most of us learn many lessons in the process of deciding who we want to be, what we want to do, and how to go about getting that job. Ann learned that the art of listening, accepting help, and exploring options was perhaps more important than committing inflexibly to one path.

LISA SIDEBAR

It's definitely important to understand what kind of work will truly satisfy you and keep you challenged. However, it usually takes some maneuvering and compromise to get there. Passion alone is not enough. Once you identify the kind of work that will make you happy, you must also find out what you need beyond your passion for it. What experience, skills, and knowledge must you acquire in order to enter that role? If you're passionate about working in a particular role, it is your responsibility to prepare for it.

In the world we live in now, the essential skills are relevance, flexibility, and lifelong learning. If you want long-term career success and financial security in retirement, you have to avoid these traps.

And that's where the fun really begins . . .

CHAPTER 3
NEW MINDSETS

The universe is change; our life is what our
thoughts make it.

—*Marcus Aurelius*

In order to change your career or plans for retirement, you have to change your behaviors. And behavior change is always preceded by a shift in mindsets.

Mindsets—how we think about everything—drive our behaviors and, ultimately, our results. Everything that's true about your results has been driven by your mindsets. The first step in changing your future—in fact, in making any change—is to shift to new mindsets.

FIRE YOURSELF! MINDSET #1:
I AM IN CONTROL OF MY OWN FUTURE.

The first mindset shift is being accountable for the results and success in your life. If you want something to change, you can make that happen. You do not need—nor should you wait for—others to take the first step. If you are not fully happy or fulfilled, it's your job to do something about it.

While it's true that you don't always have control over the events that occur in your life, you do have control over how you respond to them. How you think about an event and how you choose to respond will determine your results. And those results can lead you to the future you want to have.

LISA SIDEBAR

Laura had been a graphic designer in an ad agency for over five years. It was a very political workplace, and Laura did not like the near-constant self-promotion and competition for plum assignments. Over a glass of wine one night, Laura was again complaining about her job to a close friend. After listening to Laura for the better part of an hour, the friend interrupted her and said, "Laura, all you ever talk about is what is being done to you. You seem to think that you have no say in this. If you don't like how people are treating you, tell them to stop!"

At first Laura thought her friend just didn't understand what it was like to work at her firm. But after mulling it over for a few days she began to notice that she was not telling people what she wanted. She just complained when things didn't happen the way she thought they should— but nobody had known what she thought in the first place. When she started to look at her work through that lens, she started seeing her own part in her unhappiness. If she was going to be successful, she was going to have to both think and act differently. She returned to work determined to dump the victim mentality and advocate for herself.

FIRE YOURSELF! MINDSET #2:
IT CAN HAPPEN TO ME.

The second mindset shift is accepting that you are not immune from the forces we have discussed previously. Everything—and everyone—is subject to change. Denial is not a mindset that leads to success. If you don't believe it can happen to you, you'll miss the clues. Acceptance of today's work and retirement realities allows you to begin to look for options and possibilities.

Lynne's Story

Lynne ran a department with eight direct reports. She was a master of delegation, which she viewed as empowering her team. And her team liked working for her. Over and over, Lynne was told to develop her people and delegate work to do that development, and to make her own role more efficient. Developing leaders hear that message often.

When the organization chose to restructure and cut budgets, Lynne's position was eliminated and her team was split into two groups of four that reported directly to her boss. Lynne had prioritized developing her people, and she was respected and cherished for it. But at the end of the day, Lynne didn't look for more work to replace the tasks she appropriately offloaded to her team, leaving her with little direct work and a very compelling case for eliminating her position.

In the end, her strength at delegation was the very thing that led to her dismissal. The lesson here is that you must constantly appraise the value of your position to the organization and develop that value in order to stay relevant.

FIRE YOURSELF MINDSET #3:
I ALWAYS HAVE CHOICES.

The third mindset shift is away from a victim mentality and toward the belief that there are always choices for you to make. How you think and how you respond are always in your control. Being mindful and making conscious choices is the pathway to creating the future you really want.

People often make a mistake in attaching themselves to a specific leader. They focus on becoming one leader's go-to person, and as beneficial as that can be, it also has pitfalls.

APRIL AND JOE'S STORIES

April was relatively young and inexperienced compared to her peers, but the CEO took a liking to her and gave her opportunities and special projects. Though her peers questioned her abilities, April was confident that she was valued by the CEO and didn't worry about what others thought. April spent several years attached to corporate development projects, strategic initiatives, and many other assignments that others wished they'd landed.

Then, without warning, the CEO was fired. The new CEO did not hold April in the same high esteem. The new opportunities and strategic assignments no longer came her way. She didn't enjoy her work as much, and her performance reflected it. In a very short time, April went from being certain about her future to being concerned about it. Too late, April learned that she had to provide value to the entire organization, not just one person, and that she needed to network beyond her own organization.

Joe, on the other hand, was promoted to regional sales manager after four years as a salesperson. He was younger than most of the people he managed, and Joe's boss told him that while she would not micromanage him, she expected him to "right the ship."

Several of Joe's former peers, now his direct reports, told him they were glad someone who understood all their challenges was now in charge. However, they also believed that there was no need to make any changes because things were working fine. But Joe didn't want to settle for fine; he wanted great.

Despite knowing that he could potentially alienate his entire team, Joe reassigned accounts, put new measures in place for account reviews and forecasting, established greater accountability standards, and even hired some new, fresh salespeople who were hungrier than anyone else on the team. In short, Joe turned everything on its head.

Did all of Joe's changes work? Of course not. But Joe adjusted accordingly and kept some of the changes in place while tweaking or discontinuing others. The team increased production—and improved morale. Joe began to get calls from people in the industry asking if he had any openings. In short, Joe created success and others wanted a part of it.

FIRE YOURSELF MINDSET #4
I WANT TO LEARN AND GROW.

The fourth mindset shift is responding to and preparing for change by embracing continual learning and growth. You are never done learning and growing, especially in the constantly changing world we find ourselves in. If you aren't learning new things—if you aren't growing your skills and abilities—you won't just stay where you are. You'll fall behind. This mindset allows you to take action to move toward the future you really want.

Gary's Story

Gary is a client with a strong entrepreneurial sense. He sold off his first business after growing tired of the industry and then started up another business, one that inspired passion and energy in him.

In five years, he took it from an infant state to the third-largest provider in his niche. He was nimble and unafraid to take risks, and very wary of big companies and bureaucracy that got stuck in protocols and layers of management. Riding the thrill of his success, he felt the rest of his career would be spent in this industry.

But when Lisa met Gary, he was struggling to find a way to stay relevant in his business. Eighteen months earlier he had sold the company to a larger strategic buyer. The choice had been difficult, but he thought it the right one for himself, his employees, and his family as well as his customers. His new partner and majority owner was a big player in a tangential business that wanted to get involved with Gary's customer base. It was a perfect fit . . . at first. But six months into the new ownership, it became clear that Gary was no longer in charge. Though he wasn't yet willing to give up the reins, the new company asked him to operationalize the business. Gary resisted the idea at first, but he soon realized that the way he ran a business employing twenty people was not going to work with more than a hundred employees in locations across the country. Change was necessary to survive at this size.

Shortly after this realization, Gary began trying to collaborate with his new partners . . . but it was too late. The CEO approached Gary and told him they needed someone who could strategically lead and operationalize the business as it continued to grow. Gary was asked to step down into a product development VP role. He was a small fish in a big pond now, and he really missed the little pond.

In the end, Gary learned a hard lesson: either stick with what you know or recognize that new challenges require a willingness to grow, learn, and ask for help. Gary realized that he needed help deciding what was next and got in touch with Lisa. He went on to start a new business, knowing that his strength was in entrepreneurship and creating, not operationalizing, a business.

NEW MINDSETS, NEW RESULTS

Notice that all of the *Fire Yourself!* mindsets are "I" statements. Rather than focusing on all the things (and people) you would like to change, these mindsets allow you to use your energy to change yourself: how you think, how you respond, how you "show up" in the world.

At their core, these mindsets are all about taking personal responsibility for your career and your future.

After all, it's your life. How do you want it to turn out?

THE *FIRE YOURSELF!* PROCESS

The best way to predict the future
is to create it.
—*Peter Drucker*

At its core, the *Fire Yourself!* process requires answering four simple but crucial questions:

- Where am I now?
- Where do I want to go?
- How can I best get from here to there?
- What skills or credentials do I need next?

Whatever your present situation—ready to move on, fairly satisfied and looking to change, or simply wanting to be prepared—these questions are the key to unlocking your path forward.

The *Fire Yourself!* process uses these questions to understand what is, what could be, and what it will take to bridge the gap between them. Here's how it works:

STEP 1: WHO I AM NOW

In this step, you address the first question with an honest and comprehensive examination from three different perspectives:

- How you see things
- How others see things
- How your organization, industry, and the world at large see things

STEP 2: WHERE I WANT TO GO

In this step you address the question of where you would like to be from the same three perspectives in order to define your desired future.

STEP 3: BRIDGING THE GAP

In this step, you determine how to get from where you are to where you want to go and prioritize the actions required to reach your desired future.

Here's a visual way to look at the *Fire Yourself!* process:

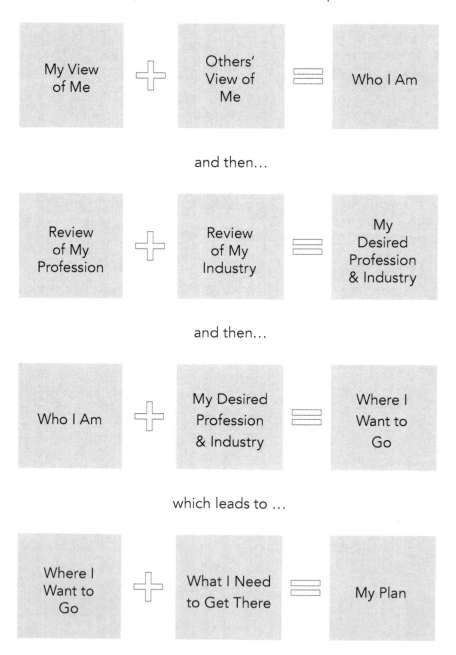

My View of Me + Others' View of Me = Who I Am

and then...

Review of My Profession + Review of My Industry = My Desired Profession & Industry

and then...

Who I Am + My Desired Profession & Industry = Where I Want to Go

which leads to ...

Where I Want to Go + What I Need to Get There = My Plan

We hope we've made the case that in today's ever-changing world, the wise course is to be continually planning in order to prevent being caught off-guard. Whatever your sense of urgency, the time to start the *Fire Yourself!* process is now.

Consider this question:

If you found out tomorrow that it was time for a change, would you be ready?

Even if you want to stay in your current job, organization, or industry, the *Fire Yourself!* process prepares you for changes within it by knowing how you can best contribute. That's good for you, but it's also good for your organization. When you understand how you provide value, you can take advantages of opportunities where what you offer is most valued. Those may be within your organization or industry, or somewhere brand new.

LISA SIDEBAR

I've worked with clients who always seem to be unsettled in their careers: they keep moving from job to job, sometimes by choice, but more often after their company decided it was time for them to leave. They never really find their niche and never really love their job.

The problem is they simply don't know—or haven't taken the time to find out—what they really want to do.

People can always tell when you don't have it figured out. You have to do your homework to find out what you're good at and what work you really want to do. When you do that, people will see your confidence.

And if you're unsettled, they see that too.

An executive once told us that, in today's world, you have to be a trapeze artist. You can't hang on to one trapeze, even if you want to. You have to move to the next trapeze, and it's easier if you're ready to jump before you have to.

We all know people who have left their jobs, either by their choice or someone else's, and said, "Now I can pursue my dreams."

Our question is, why wait? Start your pursuit right now.

CHAPTER 4

WHO AM I NOW?

Make it thy business to know thyself,
which is the most difficult lesson in the world.
—Miguel de Cervantes

Imagine it: you showed up to work only to find that, for some reason or other, your services were no longer required. What next?

Starting the journey toward your future requires a clear understanding of your point of departure: who you are now. This is a comprehensive examination of your current situation: your work, your personal life, your financial situation and—most importantly—yourself.

LISA SIDEBAR

We all have our thing. Have you ever worked with someone who thought they were skilled at something that in actuality they were not?

A great example is the sales guy who thinks he is an amazing sales guy. He is so very confident, and that confidence comes shining through to everyone, including his customers. The problem is that his confidence shows up as arrogance, and people just don't like to be around him. The irony is, he is so confident in his abilities that he cannot listen to anyone who tries to help him see it's a problem.

When you go through this process, you are going to learn what your thing is.

YOUR PERSPECTIVE

The first part of this step walks you through a self-examination of how you see your current situation: your skills, talents, experience, and so on. Be as objective as possible to avoid getting caught up in old mindsets and behaviors.

The second part focuses on how you "show up," especially at work. Do you show up in a way that creates the impression you want? Are you seen and experienced by others as your best self? Are you showing up as who you are and want to be, or as who you used to be?

Consider both your work and personal life and complete the following worksheet.

SIDEBAR

The worksheets, along with additional information, are also available for download at our website, FireYourselfNow. com.

WORKSHEET
My Perspective

Part 1: My Current Situation

What are my skills and talents? What am I good at?

What is my experience?

What knowledge do I possess?

What are my strengths?

What areas do I need to pay attention to or develop?

What brings me joy or happiness?

What is the fun in my life?

Part 1: My Current Situation

What's important to me? What do I value?

What is my value to my job, my organization, my industry, my friends and family, the world at large?

What is my reputation? How do others talk about me?

Are my experience, knowledge, and skills being fully utilized and appreciated?

What is the true value in the workplace of my experience, knowledge, and skills? (Are you marking yourself to market?)

What is my current financial situation?

What do I like best about my current situation?

Part 1: My Current Situation

What do I like least?

Part 2: How I Show Up

What does my appearance say about me?

What does my language say about me?

How do I interact with others?

What does my workspace look like?

What is my track record of performance?

What feedback have I received from my managers?

Part 2: How I Show Up

What were the results of my latest performance review or 360°
feedback process?

VALUES

We all hold different beliefs about what is important and this rein-
forces the principles of wrong and right in our life. These are our
core values. Examples of core values include:

- Dependability
- Reliability
- Loyalty
- Commitment
- Open-mindedness
- Consistency
- Honesty
- Efficiency
- Innovation
- Creativity
- Humor
- Fun-loving

Values are personal. They are not to be judged, but they are to
be honored. If you know that you care very much about loyalty,
for example, then it is important that you make choices to work in
places that support that value and to have a leader who supports
loyalty and understands what it looks like for you when it works
and when it is out of alignment. When a core value is honored,
it can motivate you to do your best work. But when it is missing
or even devalued in some way, it can cause you to be frustrated
and unproductive. Even worse, if you are not clear about what

your values truly are, you might not even know the reason you are frustrated.

Tom's Story

Tom worked as a corporate trader in an equity firm. When he started, his boss, David, really seemed to support him. If Tom needed something, David was there. If Tom made a mistake, David let him know it was a problem and clearly stated what needed to change, and then they moved on, with no more mention of the mistake. After about six months, David took a new job, and the company hired someone new from the outside. The new manager, Scott, had a very different style. Scott told Tom he was "his guy" and that he knew that Tom, who had one of the highest volumes on the trading desk, would "take care of him."

Tom kept working as he always had, but after a few weeks, he felt like he was in a funk. He was moodier and just less happy to be there. He found himself being cautious in a way that he had never been before. Shortly after that, the trader who had previously been the third-highest producer was asked to leave the firm because he had brought too much risk and his revenue was slipping. This guy had been a steady top-of-the-heap producer for years, but one bad month and he was gone. Tom realized that Scott was watching everything like a hawk, but not really talking to the traders. His words said he had their backs—that they were all "his guys"—but his actions said nothing like it. Tom realized that the company might not be the best place for him any longer.

Tom strongly valued transparency and loyalty. When Scott stopped supporting those values, Tom's attitude and behavior shifted in response to the lack of support—and he wasn't even aware of it until something significant happened.

If you know what you value, you can stand up for it. If you don't, your chances of finding the culture and environment you need go down dramatically.

WORKSHEET
Identifying My Values

Try the following two exercises to determine your values.

Part 1: Best Experiences

What are the top three experiences you have had in your career?

For each of these experiences individually, what principles, values, or emotions were present? Make a list for each experience.

Part 2: Worst Experiences

What are your worst three career experiences?

For each of those experiences individually, what principles, values, or emotions were present or absent?

The first list reflects values you desire or perhaps even require in your life and career. The second list reflects what you need to watch out for and protect yourself against.

OTHER PERSPECTIVES

To get a broader and more accurate picture of where you are now, it's important to include other perspectives. Next, you'll enlist others to help answer the previous questions, including:

- Friends
- Family
- Coworkers
- Clients
- Your manager or supervisor

The goal is to get as many perspectives as possible. You want to discover if you have blind spots about yourself and your current situation. It can be challenging to get this kind of information, but more clearly and completely you understand where you are, the better you can move forward.

People usually feel very uncomfortable having "perspective" conversations with others. We can tell you from personal experience that there is a way to conduct these conversations that will leave you feeling empowered and confident. If you approach people by telling them you are working on developing yourself, people see that as positive, character-building, and even brave work. And this is why they will not only want to help you, but are also likely do so in a way that is honest, constructive, AND affirming.

LISA SIDEBAR

When I begin a coaching relationship with clients, I start by talking to their peers, direct reports, and leader to get an understanding of what it is like to work with them. Every time, my clients learn that they are not perceived the way they think they are. Sometimes the difference is slight, but often it is a big gap. Best of all, we usually find information confirming that there is some behavior preventing the client from being more successful and plenty of information praising work or behavior the client didn't realize anyone noticed or valued. It then helps them figure out what people are paying attention to and what they are not.

We can work with the same people for years, never fully understanding that the impact we think we're having is not the impact we are actually having. If we don't understand this difference, we can try very hard and still end up making the wrong impact. Conversely, if we do understand this difference, we can make adjustments to get the impact we really want.

We all have blind spots around the perceptions that others hold. It doesn't matter if those perceptions are accurate or not; a person's perceptions are their reality.

Here's how it goes:

Start with a person you really trust and have some history with in the work world. Schedule a meeting for this conversation—offer to treat them to coffee or lunch if appropriate. You won't remember everything, so bring the Perspectives Worksheet.

Begin the conversation by explaining that you are doing some exploration around your overall career, thinking about what you are doing now and what you want to do in the future. Explain that you want to be sure you stay relevant and challenged in your work. You will be surprised at how this resonates with others. If you see it resonating with the person across from you, ask them if they wonder about this as well. The best way to get someone to want to help you is to have them appreciate what you are doing, whether they have done so already or realize they should.

Once you have discussed this, talk about your process. Explain that you want to really understand how you show up: what people appreciate and what you may do unintentionally that gets in your way. When you explain this, you must be genuine. If you are going to ask for the truth, you need to convince people you really want it.

Say things like, "You know me well, and I truly respect your opinion. I want you to feel comfortable telling me what you think about or have experienced with me. I want to learn about how others experience me and see where it overlaps with how I intend to act and where it doesn't. I am going to ask a series of people that I have different sorts of interaction with in work and my personal life. I am hoping that when I put this all together it will help me see where I am successful and where I have some opportunities."

Once you feel that you have explained the process, take them through each question from your worksheet.

IMPORTANT: You have asked for feedback; you have not invited a debate. After asking each question, be sure to listen. If you don't understand, ask clarifying questions. Do not defend or push back on what they say. Remember: this is their perspective, and it is not for you to agree or disagree. It's simply for you to learn.

Here's an example:

Question: "What do you see as areas I need to pay attention to or develop?"

Answer: "Well, if I had to come up with something, I guess I would say that you tend to avoid conflict. You are such a nice person that I think you let your people get away with more than you should."

DO Say: "Can you give me an example of where I do that?"

DON'T Say: "I know, but I have had bosses like that, and I guess maybe I'm overcompensating."

When you respond by justifying or being defensive, you are not inviting helpful dialogue. By asking a clarifying question, you show that you are listening and want to learn and grow.

Once you have gotten through all of the questions, give a hearty thank-you. If you can, genuinely convey to this person that you appreciate the good and constructive things they had to say. By having this conversation, you will create or reinforce a huge supporter, someone who will tell it like it is going forward. This person will now want to see you succeed.

When you're finished with your discussion, review what you've heard, spend some time with it, and check it out with others.

You can use the worksheet on the following pages to capture other perspectives. Make as many copies as you need.

LISA SIDEBAR

Don't be shy about asking for help. Many people are nervous or uncomfortable asking others to support them. Whether you are looking for input from a mentor or for someone who is a peer, you are telling that person you respect them enough to ask them for help. That is a compliment. Most people I know love being told that what they have to say is important. As long as you truly want the input or mentoring, you are showing respect by asking them to help you.

WORKSHEET
Other Perspectives

Part 1: Best Experiences

What do you see as my skills and talents? What am I good at?

What is your view of my experience?

What knowledge do you believe I possess?

What do you see as my strengths?

What areas do I need to pay attention to or develop?

Part 1: Best Experiences

What seems to bring me joy or happiness?

What do you think is the fun in my life?

What would you say is important to me? What do I value?

What do you see as my value to my job, my organization, my industry, my friends and family, and the world at large?

How would you describe my reputation? How do others talk about me?

Do you believe my experience, knowledge, and skills are being fully utilized and appreciated?

Part 1: Best Experiences

What is your view of the true value in the workplace of my experience, knowledge, and skills? (Am I marking myself to market)?

What is your view of my current financial situation?

What do you think is best about my current situation?

What do you think is worst about my current situation?

Part 2: How I Show Up

What does my appearance say about me?

What does my language say about me?

How would you describe how I interact with others?

How would you describe my workspace?

What is my track record of performance?

What feedback would you give me?

MAKE THE MOST OF OTHER PERSPECTIVES

When you feel you have connected with several people over this conversation, you might establish a personal board of directors, made up of people that you respect, who will be truthful and constructive with you. These are people who can truly be helpful now and in the future. They can give you feedback on where you are now as well as advice on where you could go.

Having a mentor is another way to expand your thinking. Look for someone who is a role model for how you would like to be, and use them as a sounding board and advisor. This is a great relationship that allows you to get advice from someone who has been to places and done the things to which you aspire. In that relationship you can learn valuable lessons about mistakes and successes your mentor has had. A mentor can also help you think about expanding your network and connect you to new people that will be helpful in this process. Remember that mentor relationships develop over time; don't expect a new connection to leap into the role. Rather, use your perspective conversation as a springboard to getting further feedback.

Finally, use the material that already exists. Examine documents that may provide insights, such as performance reviews, e-mails from clients and coworkers, and any documents that may provide additional answers to the "Where Am I Now?" questions.

PUT IT ALL TOGETHER

Once you've gathered all of this information, take a look at the overall picture that emerges, using the following worksheet.

Examples of completed worksheets are available on our website, FireYourselfNow.com.

WORKSHEET
Who I Am

Part 1: Review
Review all of the information you've gathered and identify the following:

Consistent themes:

Differences between your perspective and that of others:

SURPRISES
Part 2: Descriptive Paragraphs
Write short paragraphs or bulleted lists that describe the following:

Who I am at work (my value and contribution):

SURPRISES
Part 2: Descriptive Paragraphs
Write short paragraphs or bulleted lists that describe the following:

What I bring to the party (skills, knowledge, experience):

What makes me unique:

What's important to me:

SURPRISES

Part 2: Descriptive Paragraphs
Write short paragraphs or bulleted lists that describe the following:

What I have accomplished:

When you're done with this worksheet, you'll have a complete picture of who you are now.

And you're ready to look at where you want to go.

CHAPTER 5

WHERE DO I WANT TO GO?

My interest is in the future because I am
going to spend the rest of my life there.
—Charles Kettering

Once you know who you are, the next step is to decide where you want to go. For the purposes of this exercise, you're not tied to a company or role, so all choices are open to you. It's not important to be objective or realistic here. This is the place for dreaming, for aspiration, for intention.

Think of your future as a blank canvas, unsullied by what's true today. Let your imagination run wild. Be driven by what you really want, not what you think is "realistic" or "possible." Imagine that your future can be whatever you want it to be. Because it can.

At this point, you have more experience, more knowledge, more clarity, and more networking support. Now's the time to start thinking bigger.

CREATING YOUR FUTURE

Here's an activity to help you get out of what is and think creative-ly about what could be. In this process, you imagine yourself in a future where you are living the life you want, and then describe all of the ways you made that happen.

You'll need a stack of sticky notes, a pen, and a large white-board or blank sheet of paper on a wall. This exercise requires quiet space and unconstrained time. YOU are trying to imagine what the future could be, so being caught up in the present and its constraints or problems will not allow you to think of what might be. Find a space where you will not be interrupted. Turn off your phone and shut out as much outside noise as possible.

Follow the instructions on the worksheet, and remember: don't be held back by what is possible or not, what is easy or difficult. Simply imagine that you have achieved everything you really want.

WORKSHEET
Creating My Future Process

Answer the following questions to begin defining your future, a future in which anything is possible:

How do I define happiness?

In my work:

In my retirement:

In my personal life:

What do I really enjoy doing: hobbies, activities, dreams?

What skills do I most enjoy using at work?

If I were twenty-five years old and starting my career again, what would I do? (Remember, no constraints.)

This next exercise can be done alone, but you might also benefit from having someone ask you the questions and record your answers, so you are free to muse without having to write or type.

Imagine that it's five years from today. You are living the life you really want; you have achieved all of your goals: personally, professionally, and financially. You have surprised yourself by surpassing all your measures of success. When you go to work, you know you will have challenging and meaningful tasks that truly play to your strengths. And when you come home, you feel accomplished and know that you are doing the work you were meant to do.

Answer the following questions, writing your answers on sticky notes (one answer per note). Let your imagination run wild. What are all the things that are now true? Write as many ideas as possible for each question. The goal is quantity, not quality, so don't edit or restrict yourself. Reread the above paragraph and then answer the following questions:

What am I doing?

What does it look like?

How do I talk about it?

How do others talk about it?

What are the sources of my happiness?

How am I utilizing my skills, knowledge, and experience?

What have I continued to do?

Where am I?

What have I accomplished?

Who am I with?

How am I creating joy in my life?

How do I make the most of them?

What am I doing that is different than today?

What have I stopped doing?

To make sense of all of this, you will need to organize your thoughts and ideas. Start by putting the sticky notes on a whiteboard. Now notice how some of the ideas seem related. Cluster those ideas together. Don't worry if they don't all naturally cluster. Each one matters, even if it is on its own.

For each cluster, create a one-word headline and write one or two sentences that capture the flavor of the cluster. The result is a picture of your desired future.

	Headline	Description
Cluster:		
Cluster:		
Cluster:		
Cluster:		
Cluster:		
Cluster:		

	Headline	Description
Cluster:		
Cluster:		

Now look back. Did you miss anything? You may or may not choose to pursue all of these potential goals. This sheet is meant to spur your thinking and remind you about what you want. The key is to get everything you thought of in the exercise down on paper. These things came up for a reason. Embrace the ideas: they are a compass to point you in the right direction.

When you review this worksheet, it should help you understand what you have that you want, and what you need to drive toward because you don't have it yet. When you read these clusters, notice how emotionally attached you are to the ideas. The more positive the emotion you notice, the more you should follow that idea.

OTHER FUTURE PERSPECTIVES

It's important to look beyond yourself to see what the future may hold for your organization, your industry, and the world around you. Completing the following worksheet will help you see where you could go, whether it's within your current profession or industry or in another place.

Return to the people who helped you determine your current situation. Ask them where they see opportunities for you that fit with what you want to do and be.

WORKSHEET
Industry and Profession Review

What does my profession need now?

What will it need in the future?

Where is my industry now? Where will it be in the future?

What does the world need now? What will it need in the future?

PUTTING THE PIECES TOGETHER

Now that you have looked at who you are and thought a bit about your external landscape, you have some facts. Next, we'll think about what this information means and ask some of the tough questions. Doing this—and doing it well—requires total honesty. No one else has to see this. If you do it honestly, it will inform the answers to the key questions ahead: where do you want to go, and what do you want to do?

WORKSHEET
Where I Want to Go

Answer each of the following:
Do I want to change my job?
Do I want to work for my current company?
What skills do I want to use?
What jobs sound interesting to me (regardless of qualifications)?
Is there another industry that may suit me?

Answer each of the following:
What skills are most satisfying for me?
What kind of culture do I desire?
What do people most value from me?
What change is required for me to be challenged?
What change is required for me to have the compensation I desire?

After you complete this, walk away and come back to it. This is you directing your future, so don't rush it! This is the articulation of what your future opportunities will be. It might feel very broad, and that's okay. As you start navigating the process, you will see things more clearly. Some people at this point are very confident about what they want to do, down to the exact job. Most people are not, and this exercise helps them see what skills they want to use, what culture they want to participate in, and—also important—what they do not want to do and what cultures they are not suited to. This worksheet will give you enough information to know the pieces of the puzzle. You can now determine an action plan for getting there.

CHAPTER 6
BRIDGING THE GAP

The future is called "perhaps," which is the
only possible thing to call the future.
And the important thing is not to allow
that to scare you.
—*Tennessee Williams*

To move toward your optimal future, you must analyze the gap between where you are now and where you want to be. The gap can be between:
- What you are currently doing and what you want to do.
- The experience, knowledge, skills, and credentials you currently have and the ones you want or need to have.
- How you currently feel and how you want to feel.
- Your current financial state and how you want it to be.

The process of gap analysis is simply comparing what is true now and what you want to be true in the future and identifying the differences. Gaps come in many forms:
- Experience, knowledge, and/or skills
- Attitudes and behaviors
- Resources (e.g., time and cost)

Each gap must be addressed: what is required, how it can be achieved, how long it will take, and how much it will cost.

For example, let's say your optimal future requires a skill that you don't currently have. Bridging that gap will require you to identify how you will acquire that skill: a book, a seminar, coaching, and so on. Next, you have to identify how much it will cost and how long it will take.

Translating your experience into numeric form might feel awkward or inauthentic at first, but keep at it. This isn't a scorekeeping exercise. Rather, it's a way of using the subjective knowledge you've gathered so far to lay out an actionable plan for getting to where you want to be.

SIDEBAR

There is an example of a completed Personal Gap Analysis Process at www.fireyourselfnow.com

WORKSHEET
Personal Gap Analysis

Step 1   **Review What You've Written**
Review the Who I Am, Where I Want to Go, and Values worksheets from the last two chapters. These are the descriptions of where you are now and where you want go.

Step 2   **Identify What's Needed**
Examine the idea future you sketched out there and, in the worksheet below, list the experience, knowledge, and/or skills that it requires.

Step 3   **Assess Your Current State**
Enter the experience, knowledge, and/or skills that you currently have.

Step 4   **Compare the Lists**
You want to identify the following:

Required Skills	My Current Experience, Knowledge, and/or Skills	Experience, Knowledge, and/or Skills I DON'T currently have:
	Skill Level: • • • • •	Skill Level: • • • • •

Step 5   **Assess Your Competency Level**
For the experience, knowledge, and/or skills required in the future that you CURRENTLY HAVE,
assign your level of competency on the following
four-point scale:
          4 = Excellent
          3 = Good
          2 = Needs Some Improvement
          1 = Needs Much Improvement

Important Safety Tip: If you marked yourself to
market and included the assessment of others,
your numbers will be more accurate.

Step 6   **Prioritize the Actions**
Prioritize the skills you identified as needed as well
as the skills you have but may need to strengthen.
Do this in terms of their importance to achieving
your optimal future, as well as their degree of difficulty (amount of effort, time, resources).

Your actions will fall into the following four general
categories:
1. HIGH Importance and LOW Difficulty.
2. HIGH Importance and HIGH Difficulty.
3. LOW Importance and LOW Difficulty.
4. LOW Importance and HIGH Difficulty.

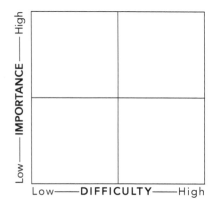

Step 7   Create Your Action Plan

Start with the actions that are HIGH in Importance and LOW in Difficulty. This will allow you to get some quick wins.

Action Item	Description of Required Action	Starting Date	Ending Date	Costs	Individuals with this Skill

As you complete each action, move to your next priority. You may be able to take multiple actions at the same time, but keep in mind that it's better to complete one action well than to have several actions that are incomplete.

LETTING GO

The Personal Gap Analysis process is focused on improving or adding competencies. But there is one other important consideration as you bridge the gaps toward your optimal future:

What are you willing to let go of to get what you want?

Remember, this is about getting you to the life that you want to have. Getting there may mean releasing some long-held assumptions or expectations. It may mean admitting, perhaps even with relief, that you don't actually want to be in the place you've been trying to reach. It may mean deciding between two possible goals, dropping one pursuit so that you can put your full resources behind achieving the other. It may mean reevaluating your priorities and making a couple of hard decisions. But unless your goal is to maintain exactly what you have now—and we hope that you understand by now just how unlikely that is to happen—some things are going to change. Embrace that fact!

Susan's Story

Susan was an executive for a small, privately owned business. She had a strong track record as a rising star in previous positions, and she saw an opportunity to rise again in a new role, this time to the CEO level. She knew she would have to work hard and earn her stripes, but the payoff would be worth it.

Susan felt consistently able to take steps forward. The problem was that she also had to take steps backward, and at times it was hard to see which direction was winning. Slowly but surely she began to notice gaps. For example, she was not fully aligned with the company's values. At the same time, she had champions who told her to keep fighting the battle. Close friends often heard Susan say, "I'm going to give it six more months." Six months later she would be saying the same thing.

Susan was financially successful, and she believed that if she just hung in there a little longer she could make the changes necessary to influence a new way of doing things. She felt this would make the culture more palatable and, therefore, help her to feel that she was an important part of the company.

As much as Susan struggled internally, she continued to tell herself, "It'll get better; I'll give it six more months." But things didn't get better. Six months became twelve months, and yet the same challenges, the same problems, continued. She was frustrated with the decisions made by her peers and the CEO, as well as with how those decisions got made. But Susan simply couldn't let go.

Eventually, the decision was made for her. The CEO decided that Susan wasn't on the bus, and they needed someone who played well with the rest of the team. Susan was given a severance package and asked to leave.

Though she felt a certain relief, Susan also regretted that she hadn't been proactive and left on her own terms. As she struggled with unemployment and finding a new job, she realized that the time and energy she had invested in hanging on would've been better used to find a new and more rewarding position.

Often, you have to put down something to pick up something new. Some of the experience, knowledge, or skills that have served you in the past will be unnecessary—or even harmful—in the future. To move forward, you have to be willing to let go of the mindsets and behaviors that are preventing you from having the joy, the purpose, the fulfillment—the life—you really want.

CHAPTER 7

YOU *CAN* GET THERE FROM HERE

Life is trying things to see if they work.

—*Ray Bradbury*

Once you've fired yourself, whatever the specifics of your action plan, carrying it out means you are now in the Change business. Moving in new directions toward your optimal future requires you to think differently, act differently, and perhaps even look differently.

SHOWING UP STRONG

Whether or not your current role is in question, take a moment to think about how you would show up physically if you were interviewing tomorrow. Are you putting your best self forward every day, or have you gotten a bit complacent? You spent the last few chapters articulating where you want to be: are you showing up in ways that will move you toward that goal?

As you embark on your new adventure, getting in shape, updating your wardrobe, and getting a new haircut are all simple yet effective ways to demonstrate to the world that you are serious about making changes. They provide some of those "quick wins" we discussed earlier: solid steps you can easily take that give you momentum for the larger tasks in your action plan.

Dressing for success is more than a cliché . . . it's a fact of life. If two people with equal capabilities are being evaluated for a new job or promotion, the one who dresses well and with professional presentation will win out over the one who dresses poorly or too casually. It is a fact that many people have been given an opportunity because they looked the part. Freshening up your look can make a big difference.

All of these factors affect how you are perceived by others, how you "show up" both personally and professionally. Less easy to manage are how others perceive your attitude and behavior. Success in any career requires skill at your job, true, but also the ability to work well with other people. Focusing on just one aspect of showing up is a dangerous strategy.

TONY AND TOM'S STORIES

Everybody loved Tony, and from the first time Lisa met him, it was clear why. Social, outgoing, fun to be around, Tony was the perfect customer service guy. Throughout his ten years at the company, Tony was the guy people wanted to work with, the guy people called to find out what was going on, the guy clients appreciated.

He loved his job, but Tony wanted to do more. He felt ready to take on the next position: director of customer service. But as much as he was loved and respected in his current position, people thought the director's role was a stretch. Tony was known for his social impact, not his accomplishments. He was the life of the party, the guy everyone wanted to joke around with and join for a drink. While Tony was a part of conversations about the direction of the company and business strategy, no one ever saw him leading those conversations. People remembered Tony's funny jokes and welcoming demeanor. While it made him likable and even sought after, it didn't create confidence in his ability to lead.

But it was difficult for Tony to see what was clear to everyone else, and so it was nearly impossible for him to figure out how to change and be seen differently.

In contrast, Tom was considered a rock star as an accountant. He was given more and more responsibilities and was wildly successful time after time. Tom had spent a lot of time in his industry: he was good, and he knew it. And he made sure everyone else knew it, too. He soon got a reputation as a know-it-all, someone who always believed he was right and wouldn't take input from anyone else. Meetings with Tom were an ordeal that nobody enjoyed . . . except for Tom.

When a new boss took over the department, she soon found herself spending significant time and energy dealing with Tom's effects on the rest of the team. As good as he was, the way Tom showed up was preventing the department from achieving their results, and when asked for ways to cut costs, she saw Tom as a liability.

And so Tom was let go, not for his personal results—which he got—but for how he got those results. He was replaced by a younger accountant who enjoyed working with the team. And without the high salary Tom commanded because of his tenure, the department got better results for less money.

As mentioned previously, we all have blind spots, and it is vital to gather the perspectives of others—a lesson Tony and Tom learned the hard way. Look back over your worksheets, especially the Surprises sections. Are you creating the impressions that you want to make? Do people enjoy working with and for you, or have your trusted sources reported some unintended, negative consequences? If so, create a plan to swiftly and actively address those problems and start showing up as your best self.

If all of your feedback has been positive, you may want to dig a bit deeper. To be clear, none of us are perfect. Unflaggingly positive feedback in real time or in this exercise suggests that people may only be telling you what you want to hear. Make sure you know what behavior to focus on and what behaviors get you in trouble, intentionally or not.

Focus on your strengths, and ask for help or find people on your team to help supplement areas that are not your strengths.

BRINGING THE PASSION

The fuel of change is passion. It's important to understand what makes you tick and what kind of work will truly satisfy you, interest you and keep you challenged. If you find work that is meaningful to you, it's possible to be more successful and have everything that goes with that success. If you feel that you're not showing up well at work, take a moment to think about what could be dragging your attitude down. Review your worksheet answers, especially the Putting the Pieces Together section in chapter 5, and your gap analysis.

Give yourself time to think about the following worksheet. You've gathered a lot of facts about yourself so far, but passion isn't something that can be described by facts.

WORKSHEET
Identifying My Passions

Once you have reviewed the previous worksheets, think about the high and low points that the information describes. Where do you feel at your best and worst? The points at which you're feeling your absolute best are moments when your work and your passion are in alignment. When you know what creates those high points, you can work toward making more of them.

Answer each of the following:
What activities or situations make me feel most energized and engaged (in and out of work)?
What activities or situations make me feel demotivated and disengaged (in and out of work)?
Where do I feel most satisfied in the value I bring?

Answer each of the following:
How can I incorporate my most energizing and satisfying pursuit into my life, both now and in the future?
Am I taking steps now toward where I want to be?
Am I excited and confident about getting there? What do I need to feel excited and confident about it?
Am I increasing the value I offer to others along the way?

The more passionate you are about your new direction, the more likely your success. And passion is highly contagious; if you are excited and confident, others will want in on the action. That's important, because you'll need the support of others on your journey.

Scott's Story

Scott is a chef who had grown up with a passion for cooking good food and dreamed of opening his own restaurant. He bought his first place, and soon became well-known both locally and nationally for his farm-to-table restaurant. But eventually, the amount of time he spent in the restaurant began to take a toll on his personal life. At the same time, he wanted to build a new revenue stream, so he took a second job as executive chef for a country club. He began to redesign the food service at the country club, and while continuing to be involved, he relied more and more on his staff to run the restaurant.

As time went on, it became clear to Scott that—though it broke his heart—he had to sell the restaurant and focus on the country club. But he was spending most of his time on entertaining and catering, and less on food . . . his true passion.

So he left for a more corporate position with a hotel. He saw it as an opportunity to get back to transforming food, but it didn't turn out as he had hoped. He was working crazy hours that kept him away from his family, and he missed the complete control he'd had previously.

And so again he left, becoming executive vice president of food for a large national food-service firm. He was in charge of all food for residence halls and sporting events at a large university, as well as food purchasing for the entire university. He rekindled his passion for good, interesting, and sustainable farm-to-table food, while having more time to spend at home with his family.

Scott started with a dream; he didn't give up on it, and through trial and error, he learned what he was good at and what was truly calling to him. He wasn't afraid to make changes, and he found a way to fully live his dream.

SHARING YOUR STORY

Now that you know who you are and where you want to be, you should have a rich variety of words to describe both. Next, you'll use these ideas and terms to start talking about yourself in ways that get you feedback and ultimately reveal what opportunities are out there. Use the ideas generated by the exercises in the previous chapters to create the next important tool in your career toolbox: your story.

Your story is the concise explanation of who you are and where you want to go. It's commonly known as an "elevator pitch": a summary that can be shared in the time span of an elevator ride.

Everyone should have a story—not just job seekers. Though it can be difficult to reduce your vision and value to a few sentences, it's important to be able to quickly and clearly give your connections a sense of you and your goals. Why? So they know how to think about you and how they can help. Knowing your story makes it easier for them to spot opportunities that may benefit you.

The more specific your story, the better. Being interested in anything and everything is not particularly helpful when trying to connect with others. Your story should focus on where you are headed and, if possible, the type of help and support you are looking for. The more and better you tell your story, the more people know how to think about you.

Your story is simply a short synopsis (thirty seconds or less) that explains:

- What you are you doing now: not just your title, but what you actually DO.
- What makes you successful: the skill that you provide or the characteristic that you are known for.
- What you want to do and are looking for: what should people be thinking about for you, the opportunity you are looking for. Describe it in a way that others will understand.

Here's an example:

I build and evaluate the financials in growth-oriented companies. I have had a great career helping companies grow and expand based on their articulated M&A strategies. Right now I am looking for an opportunity to join a growth-oriented company that wants to expand by acquisition.

Brief, clear and easy to understand. That's what makes a great elevator pitch.

Your story is told in writing, as well. Create a brief, focused written version of your story to add to social media profiles, thank-you notes, e-mails, and other written communications.

And don't forget your resume. It should be a living document, not something that gets dusted off and updated when an opportunity arises. Update your resume at least once a year, or even better, whenever you have an accomplishment or significant change in your career.

Ask several colleagues to look at your resume and give you advice. Everyone will have different viewpoints, but remember: it is your document to own. Take others' input and make it reflect you in a way that makes you feel confident.

As important as your resume may be, don't let it prevent you from taking action. Don't put off networking because you haven't finished your resume. Make the time to get it done and then move on.

The resume alone won't get you the next thing. What you say, who you say it to and how you act will do that.

FINDING YOUR GUIDES

If your life took a sudden turn tomorrow, who would you call first? Identifying those who can support your efforts is important for each step in your action plan. Who can point you in the right direction? Who has been there and can be a guide for you? Who has the information, contacts, or influence to help you achieve your vision? These are the people who need to be in your network.

If your goal is a new job or career, consider this data from the US Department of Labor:

- About 5 percent of job seekers obtain jobs through the open job market, which consists of help wanted ads, the Internet, and print publications.
- Another 24 percent obtain jobs by cold-calling companies directly.
- 23 percent obtain jobs through employment agencies, college career-services offices, and executive search firms.
- Fully 48 percent obtain their jobs through referrals or word of mouth. These individuals get the job referrals by networking.
- Whatever your desired future, a robust network is a must.

CREATIVE NETWORKING

There is networking, and there is creative networking.

The basics of networking are simple: connect with people who can help you move forward. We assume that you know the basics, and if not, there are dozens of books and articles already out there to get you going. But being truly effective means getting beyond the basics.

LISA SIDEBAR

When I tell clients they need to spend more time networking so they know what is going on and what is being said, they often look very disinterested . . . or even worried. But networking doesn't have to be difficult. The important thing to remember is that it is simply about getting to know the person across the table better than you did when you greeted them.

First of all, cast your networking "net" as broadly as possible. Make a list of previous colleagues and managers, vendors or partners in your current role, and neighbors or others in your social life who seem happy and successful in their work. Look for people in roles that you find interesting; ask about what they do and how they got into that work. You will be surprised how many networking resources you have.

The criteria for a good contact is not hard and fast. Your goal is to share your story with people who may have ideas for you. Those ideas may show up in the most obvious place, or they may come from someone you never expected.

Networking isn't selling—not when it's done right. Rather, networking is sharing information. I tell you about me and what I am up to, and you tell me about you and what you are up to. Then we see if we can help each other. If yes, great! We do that. If not, we file away the information we shared and hope that we can pass it on in a useful way to someone else.

Networking isn't just about face-to-face handshakes today. It's at your fingertips as well, through web-based social media such as LinkedIn, Facebook, and others. And it's not just who you know; it's also who knows you and who they know that you can connect with. Return to your list of contacts and expand it beyond just the people who have an immediate connection to your career: add everyone you know. Then think about who they know: who among their connections might be of help to you? Work your social media contacts, and be on the lookout for new connections.

Networking takes time: meeting with someone once may not be enough. Relationships are built over the long term, and sometimes the best results come with patience and persistence. If an initial meeting or event uncovers common goals and the potential for mutual support of each other's careers or interests, make a plan to meet quarterly or biannually to grow the relationship and keep each other in mind.

Networking isn't a quid pro quo. Sometimes you have to give, and give, and give in order to get. You may come across more opportunities to support your contacts because you're new and growing, because you have a higher-volume businesses, or because you simply like to help others. In any case, don't keep score. A single connection made after months or years of effort—and therefore based on firm and mutual trust—may be well worth cultivating the relationship. But by the same token, if there is no reciprocity, be willing to invest your time and social capital elsewhere.

JOHN SIDEBAR

Back in chapter 1 I told the story of Davis, who turned finding a job into his full-time job. Networking goals were key to his success. He set a daily goal to schedule one meeting, send one e-mail, and add one new contact.

Davis finds great comfort and strength in his faith, and he attended a church support group that not only allowed him to network with others in transition, but also provided insights from outside speakers. During one of these presentations, Davis learned that the best opportunities come three to seven layers deep into the networking process, and that his mindset had to be that he wasn't "looking for a job," he was "managing a project." The result would be his next career destination.

Davis kept those three to seven layers in mind and, holding to his daily goal, worked himself deeper down each networking trail whenever he could. Three layers deep into one trail, he found himself having coffee with a contact who told him he had just been phoned by a recruiter looking to fill a new position—one that matched Davis' qualifications and career interests. That next step led to his current role.

> The lesson is that when it comes to networking, you must set goals (daily, or at least quarterly) and then use them to go wide and deep.

Don't forget about recruiters. As we mentioned in chapter 1, they're always on the lookout for assets who will add value to their clients' businesses. They know where the jobs are and how to connect the right people with the right opportunities. Make sure they know who you are and what your optimal future looks like. But keep this in mind: recruiters aren't usually interested in talking to unemployed people. They are hired to find candidates employed at—and tested by—other organizations.

That's all the more reason to reach out and take their calls before you need them. As a friend and client used to have on his card for his bail bond business, "It's better to know me and not to need me than to need me and not to know me."

Whether or not you're considering a job change, you should be constantly expanding and deepening your network. The specific goal of networking varies for individuals, but the overall goal is twofold: be sure the person knows how to describe who you are and what you do, and be seen by the other person as successful. In other words, the key to good networking is building relationships.

To do this, you need to engage the other person. No one wants to go to coffee to listen to someone else drone on and on. However, everyone loves to see that people are interested in them. So start your meeting by asking the other person how they are and what is new, not just a cursory question, but with genuine curiosity. If there are ways you can offer help, advice, or resources, this is the time to pony up. If not, just be a good listener.

After that, it's your turn. Tell the other person what you are doing. You want to be sure that by the end of the conversation the person across the table understands what you do and what you want to do. This may not be the person to help you figure out your next move, but a week later, when they hear someone say they are looking for an excellent finance person (for example), you want to be sure they know to bring up your name.

Be prepared! If you know in advance who you are meeting, you may have categories of connections or even specific people in common, and you may thus have a chance to "feed" your network with additional connections and introductions. Consider asking for advice on how to reach out and facilitate introductions deeper into their network—with their permission, of course, and with an offer of introductions in your network if appropriate.

You don't have to ask for favors or even for leads. Now, if you are comfortable and you want to make the ask, go for it. But it's not necessary. Oftentimes just letting people know who you are and what you are looking for is enough.

The last crucial part of a networking meeting—especially one that you initiate—is to be sure to ask the other person if there is anything you can do to help them. The secret is to listen and engage the other person. If you each walk away having learned more about the other, you have both been successful.

Networking should be a way of life, not simply a job search strategy. When done well, it doesn't feel like a schmoozy sales experience; rather, it feels like you made a connection with an interesting person, and you want to see them be successful. If you are conscientious about maintaining connections, you increase your chances of finding the people who can really make a difference for you. You never know where a networking trail will lead, so the more connected you are, the better.

INTERVIEWING WITH CURIOSITY

The skills you hone in creative networking are also useful when someone requests an interview: the goal is to connect and get curious. More art than science, interviewing is an important skill whether you are seeking information or applying for a job. Successful interviewing means remembering a single fact: an interview is simply a conversation between two people to determine if an opportunity is a good fit.

Approaching any interview as a conversation immediately reduces your stress and increases your confidence. Look at it as an equal opportunity: both people have something to gain from the conversation.

In a conversation, rather than trying to impress the other person or merely answering questions, you are actively listening, responding, and asking your own questions.

That requires preparation on your part. First, identify:

- What you want to learn from the conversation.
- What you want the other person to know about you by the end of the conversation.

Next, prepare a list of questions prior to the conversation. For example, a job seeker might ask:

- After the first sixty to ninety days in this role, how will the new person be assessed?
- How will you know if you made a good hiring decision?
- What are the three most important priorities in this role?
- What's your favorite part about working here?
- Based on what you know about me, where do you think I could make a contribution?
- What makes the culture here different from other places?

You should also ask questions about the organization: the culture, what's okay and not okay, future plans, development opportunities, and so forth. The goal is to gain and share information so that both parties can assess the fit.

The idea is to make this a dialogue. You want the person on the other side of the desk to become more relaxed than formal. Once that happens, you end up having a conversation, not an interview. That allows both of you to be more casual in your comments and learn more about each other.

It's always better to ask open-ended questions—those that require more than a yes-or-no answer. They not only provide more information, but also encourage discussion and move the conversation further forward.

Never underestimate the power of well-crafted questions. They provide a strong impression of who you are and your potential value. There is nothing better than asking a thought-provoking question and having the other person say, "That's a great question. I hadn't really thought of that before."

Jack's Story

If you're on the hunt for a new position, an important piece of information to gather during an interview conversation is why the last person left the job.

The chief information officer role was open at a large pharmaceutical company, and Jack was interviewing for it with a headhunter. Jack knew there was stiff competition for the position, but he was hopeful he could show them why he was the best candidate. He had done his homework before the interview; he had reached out to colleagues who knew folks at this company, and the stories he heard were consistent. The last CIO was asked to leave, but no one was clear on why—just lots of conjecture.

Jack knew that to make the most of the interview, he needed to understand what qualities they wanted that the previous CIO had lacked. The headhunter very broadly described the role and the skill set they were looking for. Jack asked about the role's biggest challenges. Again, very broad answers. Jack then asked what was working. A long and detailed response. Jack took notes and followed up with more questions about the things that were working.

The following week Jack was asked to meet the CEO for an interview. A very direct man, the CEO asked pointed questions about Jack's previous roles. When Jack asked about the CEO's expectations of him, the answers were direct and to the point. Jack then asked if there was anything else he needed to know about how things worked there to be successful. The CEO talked frankly about his pet peeves. Based on the headhunter's comments and what the CEO had just told him, it became clear that the CEO did not like the previous CIO.

So with great candor (and courage) Jack said, "I want this job. I really want this job. At the same time, I get the feeling that you did not have a good relationship with the previous CIO. For me or anyone else to be successful, it would be helpful to understand what caused the previous CIO to not be successful in your eyes."

The CEO immediately laughed and said, "Don't worry. You have just demonstrated that it won't be a problem. The last guy didn't ever disagree with me, never questioned me. Just did what I said. That's a problem because I am not an IT expert. I need someone who will push back when necessary. I appreciate that you will."

Jack got the offer, accepted the position, and built great relationships with his boss and peers. That allowed him to make great progress in the organization.

LISA SIDEBAR

When you are going into an interview, be curious. This is an important process, and you need to be an active participant. Being professional and respectful is of the utmost importance, but that doesn't mean you don't get to ask good questions.

Finding the right questions to ask requires preparation.

Before you walk through that door, you should find out the latest news about the company, what goals it is officially pursuing, what local and national factors might have created this job opportunity (including news about the departure of any previous people in that role), and if possible, information about the role of the person or people with whom you'll interview. The more background information you can gather, the more clear a picture you'll have of who they're looking for to fill that role and why.

FINDING AND BEING A MENTOR

Mentoring is a fabulous way to gain knowledge and perspective (it should be clear at this point how important perspective is!) for people of all ages. When you ask someone to be your mentor you are asking them to share their stories of how they got to where they are and what they learned. When sharing such information, you learn to look at situations differently—and get proof that you don't already know everything.

No matter how senior you are in your career, you can always find someone more senior (even if they are now retired). There is always an opportunity to learn and get guidance from others. Thinking you are too old for a mentor is naïve. If you are about to retire, there is a retired executive or two out there who could be invaluable to you in your transition.

You can also be a mentor! If you are fresh in your career, there are college students who need guides. If you are an executive, I don't have to tell you how many young, ambitious folks are out there who could benefit from learning what it really takes to climb the corporate ladder.

As a mentor, you get to share your experience to teach others, which is very rewarding. It also helps you tap into how people in more junior roles are thinking. Not to mention that you will learn about yourself while you listen to their stories.

Mentoring is a great way to stay relevant and gain perspective all at once. Having a mentor and being a mentee throughout your career will keep you fresh, aware, and informed . . . which is a great alternative to outdated, naïve, and misinformed.

MAINTAINING YOUR ENERGY

All of the strategies discussed in this chapter are best practices for career development, whether you're happy where you are or looking for a new direction. Each should be part of your weekly or even daily habits. It might seem difficult to keep up that level of involvement, but all of these activities have the potential to become self-sustaining: done right, they will pay off in the short term as well as in longer-term preparedness.

All of the tools discussed here share a few basic elements. First—and this might sound familiar—you can't show up fully if you don't know what you want and what you're worth. That includes knowing what you can offer others, researching to find the right questions, and checking whether your outward appearance and behavior reflect what you value personally and professionally. Second, the best ways of getting known and finding opportunities involve meeting people and building respectful, two-way connections with them, getting curious, asking good questions, and finding out about what they need and how you can help each other. And third, as often as you ask for help, you can offer it to someone else down the line: whether you're passing along your mentor's advice to a mentee of your own or linking a connection to a recruiter with a good opportunity, you're laying the groundwork for future opportunities that you can't yet see.

Remember, nobody will invest more energy in you than you.

Taking the time to do it, and do it well, will get you closer to the life you want to have.

CHAPTER 8

ALIGNING YOUR RESOURCES

Don't tell me where your priorities are.
Show me where you spend your money,
and I'll tell you what they are.
—*James W. Frick*

Your current and future resources—particularly your current and future financial decisions—are a crucial component in the *Fire Yourself!* process. Our goal in discussing money here, however, is not to produce another financial planning book. That's been done. In fact, most efforts fall short—way short—because financial planning is such a personal endeavor. Mass-market approaches are doomed to failure because, by design, the author has to paint in such broad brushstrokes.

JOHN SIDEBAR

There's a new book promising a personal finance panacea every week, it seems. Selling as many copies as possible is the enemy of personalized—and therefore relevant—advice. With sales the first priority, such authors leave readers at best dissatisfied and at worst misguided as they wax on with generalities or proffer novel schemes that worked for them . . . but translate poorly outside their unique situation.

The Internet is even worse. Information is not the same as wisdom. Cyberspace has been flooded with information, but wisdom is still in short supply. Financial planning is as much about motivation and accountability—the *why*—as it is about the *how*.

Even though survey after survey shows most Americans are not working with a financial planner and are not otherwise planning on a regular basis, we assume you've got your financial house in order. (If you don't, you'll find John's contact information at the end of the book!) What we would like to do is discuss your financial preparedness as it regards career preparedness and planning.

For most of the professionals for whom this book is intended, financial success and even the creation of wealth is tied as firmly to proficient career management as it is to the proper management of assets, and vice versa. The *Fire Yourself!* process of career management will also serve you well in your approach to money and planning. In fact, the idea for this book came from our observation of the interplay between and similarities of these two aspects of our lives.

How do they work together? Well, "they" say the wealthy get

wealthier. Some whine and complain about that, and others realize it's true and act accordingly. Having your finances in order, and even striving to get ahead of the curve, expands your options when opportunities present themselves. If you're living paycheck to paycheck and have nothing in savings, you can't be prepared to jump on an opportunity to join a colleague in a speculative venture that could be the next Big Thing. Nor are you in a good position to take any chances at all, prudent or otherwise, with your career. Instead, being financially vulnerable is likely to make you feel much more dependent on your current job or occupation, even if you are underemployed or outright miserable in it, and much less likely to think beyond simply hanging on for dear life—it's literally the opposite of being financially independent.

They also say success is where opportunities and preparedness meet. If you're on track or even ahead of schedule for retirement, and if you maintain adequate savings (for most people, the cash equivalent of six to twelve months of personal or household overhead) to serve as a buffer for unplanned events or a springboard for a new venture, you are much more likely to feel comfortable taking a chance with your career.

JOHN SIDEBAR

To illustrate the importance of long-term plans, I cite a study done by CNN on the performance of the stock market. Very few rolling ten-year periods (i.e., 2001–2011, 2002–2012) and no fifteen-year rolling periods in the stock market (using the S&P 500 as a proxy) have ended with a negative result. Even more interesting is the fact that the greatest share of the positive growth in most of these periods comes from a few trading days.

For example, according to the study, had you invested $10,000 in the S&P 500 Index in 1996 and left it there, by the end of 2011 you'd have just over $22,000. If, however, you missed only the ten best trading days during that period, you'd have ended up with only half of that amount.

This might sound like I, or the faceless "they," condone timing the market, and I would agree if that were possible. Rather, it emphasizes staying invested (as in the adage, "Time in the market, not timing the market"), staying engaged, and thinking long term.

The same concept applies to John's clients' success in growing and managing their careers. Much of the success we ultimately realize in our careers can be tied to a handful of seminal events—some planned, some not. An introduction from a mutual friend, a chance meeting at an event, a casual conversation at a kid's birthday party, or being forced to make a change after getting fired or a company going out of business. Or—firing yourself!

Again, the two go hand in hand because being financially prepared leaves you much more likely to be looking for, recognize, and able to take advantage of one of these seminal events, and even one such successful move can lead to even greater financial success and preparedness. The wealthy get wealthier.

Being prepared financially means taking daily steps toward achievement of an overall plan. The strategy, the tactics, and the motivation behind both form the core of John's planning practice.

His approach to long-term planning strategy and its tactical elements, positioning assets and managing cash flow, is founded in assisting clients in becoming more aware and better informed, and in discovering and articulating their highest-held goals and dreams. With that knowledge, they become more deliberate and intentional in using their resources.

Sound familiar? At its base, this is the financial twin of Lisa's career strategies. Knowing what you really, really want gives you clarity in the pursuit of something you simply want. We believe this holds true as much for the daily and strategic actions we take to grow and manage our careers as it does our finances, and the fact that the two are so inextricably intertwined serves as the foundation for this book.

So let's explore the top-down, values-oriented steps you can take to put yourself in a position of financial strength and be better prepared to take advantage of the career-management concepts in *Fire Yourself!*

MAP OUT YOUR VALUES, DREAMS, AND GOALS

Start by mapping out the rest of your life with your spouse or life partner. Make a timeline on a piece of paper or whiteboard, and list what you would like to fill it with. More than a bucket list, this is as much about what you would like to be doing tomorrow and in the next two to five years as it is what you hope to do before you leave this earth. Think about what you enjoy doing together. Think about what you would do if time and money were no object. Think of those you care the most about and what you would like to share with or provide for them.

This will inform you of what you really, really want—what you truly value and truly enjoy doing with your time. It will help you to quantify the cash flow required to serve a more values-oriented lifestyle in the long term.

Your map will also serve to separate you from the forces of our consumption economy and the notion of pacing yourself against others and spending money on things that matter only to them. Time really is like money: whether you have a lot or a little of it isn't as important as spending it wisely and deliberately, while at the same time maximizing the joy it brings you.

JOHN SIDEBAR

> To me planning and waste are opposing forces for both time and money.

FOLLOW THE MONEY

Next, gather information from at least ninety days' worth of spending—an entire calendar year is better—sort it by simple categories, and quantify them. I suggest a few categories common to most households:

- Fixed Expenses (e.g., mortgage, insurance, car, taxes)
- Household (e.g., things you must spend money on: toiletries, school supplies, home maintenance)
- Groceries (e.g., eating in)
- Entertainment (e.g., movie theaters, eating out, bars and nightclubs)
- Discretionary (e.g., things you choose to spend money on: books, music, toys, hobbies)
- Debt (e.g., student loans, credit cards)
- Charitable contributions (e.g., monthly or yearly donations of money)

Twenty categories is too many. Three categories is too few. Try for eight to ten categories. The key is not that they match up with mine or anyone else's: rather, they must be simple and yet meaningful to you, and every single penny that goes out has a category. Ideally, all of this would be in a spreadsheet, allowing you to sort and average out your spending, gaining an understanding of where your dollars are going.

BECOME MORE DELIBERATE AND INTENTIONAL

Now, without judgment on yourself or anyone else in your household, analyze your average monthly cash flow in each category as it regards value. Ask each other, with respect and an open mind, "Are our expenditures in alignment with the map of the rest of our lives?" It's not that you can't afford $800 per month for eating out (although that may very well be the case); the question is, "Are we getting $800 of value? Is it possible we could eat out just as often, and enjoy each other's company just as much, for $500 per month?"

This step usually yields not only an analysis but also a set parameter for the future. It also gives you a process and a plan to provide ongoing feedback going forward. The mindset here is just as important as the process. Don't think of it as "going on a budget"—rather, you are simply becoming more intentional and deliberate with your cash flow. Smart is as smart does.

HIRE A COACH

Seek professional help. Work with a financial planner. It doesn't have to be John or someone from his firm, but everyone needs a coach and the guidance, objectivity, and accountability they provide. The best strategy is the one that gets done. You can't get that from a book. Not even a great book like *Fire Yourself!*

Sam and Tina's Story

Sam and Tina were referred to John by another client. At the time, Sam was a vice president at a bank and Tina was an IT consultant with a firm serving corporate clients in the region. When we met, they were in their late thirties and had three young children and a beautiful home in the suburbs. They were living the American dream in the segment of the upper middle class John calls the "Working Affluent."

John took them through his customary planning process: helped them understand their benefits and retirement plans at work, addressed their need for insurance, consolidated and reallocated their retirement and education assets, advised them on refinancing their mortgage and revising the insurance on their home and their cars, and helped them get their wills and beneficiary elections updated. They were good savers and lived well within their means intuitively, but they didn't have a handle on where their cash flow was going or where they stood for retirement and funding their children's education. After a few meetings they gained a much better understanding of the substantial financial security they had created, but it was the cash-flow exercise that had the greatest impact on their outlook.

It was then that Tina shared her dream of starting her own consulting practice. Visiting with them about this idea, John discovered that Sam was not that enthusiastic about the idea because they both had strong, stable incomes and were able to do pretty much anything they wanted financially, and he enjoyed the career security they had worked so hard to achieve together.

Tina, however, was not only producing as a consultant for her employer's firm but also bringing in much of its new business, and she had no small part in retaining their existing clients as well. She knew that the owner was profiting richly on her work; that was fine, as he had taken a chance on her years earlier. But she had grown restless and had been expressing a desire to Sam to break out on her own.

John asked Tina about the pipeline of clients she could potentially recruit in her first year. She responded that not only did she feel she had a pipeline in place, but many of her clients had also been encouraging her to pursue her dream, and she could do so without poaching any of her employer's clients—an important factor for her. Moreover, she felt she might make more money on her own, even in her first year. John noted their adequate cash savings and the understanding they had gained of their monthly household cash-flow needs, and he asked a few key questions:

1. Sam, having reviewed your cash-flow needs, do you believe

you could run your household and, with a couple tweaks, live a comfortable lifestyle on your income alone?

2. Tina, how confident are you that by the end of the first year of your new venture you could generate enough revenue to replace your current take-home income?

3. Sam, at your level in your organization, you have regular conversations with your boss about the employees who report to you, and you are constantly evaluating the organization's needs for their work, right? I suppose your boss has the same conversation about you, don't you think?

4. Tina, if you decide to wait to pursue your dream of starting your own firm until the timing might be better, what in your mind would make the timing better? "If not now, when?"

Sam seemed to get John's point: the corporate world is no more secure—in fact, it's likely less secure—than being self-employed. After visiting for a few more minutes, John reiterated the question: "Tina—if not now, when?"

Today, Sam is still happily employed at the same company. Tina broke away, started her new firm, beat her corporate salary in her first year in her new venture, and has grown her company larger than the firm she separated from. She and her past employer often refer clients back and forth and maintain a relationship of mutual respect. Her new workstyle affords her not only more income, but also a more flexible lifestyle. She is able to spend more time with her children and, of course, Sam. In their planning review meetings since, Tina credits the understanding she gained of their financial position and resources, as well as John's "prodding questions," for bridging the gap in her and Sam's confidence about pursuing her dream.

Taking the simple steps described above will give you the data to determine how much cash you should keep on hand to create a six-month (or more for certain executives and business owners) emergency fund. Determine how much you should theoretically be able to save every month to reach that goal and then to redirect those dollars to your long-term goals and dreams. You will also be able to ascertain the minimum cash flow required to run your household in the event of a career change (planned or unplanned) or an emergency. It will give you and your household a structure for financial discussions in the future and a means by which to feel much more confident as consumers. These steps may seem simplistic or even obvious . . . and yet most of us don't use them, or any process, to manage our financial resources. The wealthy get wealthier . . .

CHAPTER 9

RETIREMENT

You cannot change the facts of the past,
but you can change the meaning of the past.
—George Ellis

How do you think about retirement? Is it a shining reward that you get at age sixty-five after working for one company for many years? Is it something far off in the future that will be the result of a long—and perhaps varied—career? Is it something you don't think about at all? Or maybe it's a source of concern and worry?

Throughout history, people have thought about retirement in a remarkable variety of ways. It's worthwhile to understand the various meanings of retirement through the years to ensure that how you are thinking about retirement now is accurate.

Retirement was not always something people looked forward to. For millennia, in fact, there was no retirement. Up until less than a century ago, people worked until they either no longer could (in which case, they relied on family or charity for support) or they died. As the centuries passed, people began living longer and longer and, consequently, working longer and longer.

Eventually, this led to a problem. Older workers were holding on to their jobs, preventing younger workers from finding employment. This reached a critical point in the Great Depression, which led to Social Security—paying people to retire.

Rapid growth in employer-provided pensions followed, due to the freeze on pay increases and the need to retain workers during World War II. Workers now had financial incentives to retire at age sixty-five. Longer life spans meant that there might be years, even decades, when people didn't work, and this led to the rise of retirement communities and the notion of retirement as a time of leisure to be enjoyed.

In this environment, a typical workplace cycle went like this: you got a degree, landed a job for which the degree was designed, and began working your way up the corporate ladder. Along the way, you took vacations whose length and timing were dictated by your employer and your salary.

As your income increased (which it faithfully did, year after year), so did your estimated pension benefit, as well as your projected Social Security benefit. There were no 401(k) plans or mutual funds, so you didn't have to worry about the volatility they might inject into your retirement plan. Everything was safe and secure. As long as you did your job, played well with others, and lived to see retirement, you would indeed enjoy your golden years.

It wasn't uncommon for people to work their entire career at one company and then rely on a defined-benefit pension plan (managed somewhere upstairs) and Social Security (guaranteed money from the US government) for the majority of their retirement income.

Pension managers (those folks upstairs) had it easy: actuarial assumptions tied to a lockstep workforce meant confidently defined benefits. Senior employees retired at sixty-five, lived a relatively finite number of years beyond retirement, and were replaced at the beginning of the conveyor belt by young college graduates eager to join the ranks. As a result, pensions were well managed and well funded. Former coworkers, now retired, reported that the checks came every month like clockwork.

Social Security was backed by the full faith and financial strength of the federal government. Bolstered by a mostly booming economy and a favorable ratio of payers to payees, the system ran at a substantial surplus. (And later became a lender of trillions to the rest of the federal government, but we digress.)

Life was good. Safety and security (or at least, the appearance of safety and security) ruled the day.

Children watched their fathers (and, increasingly, their mothers) make this slow, steady, safe, and secure march through work and toward retirement. Parents encouraged their offspring to follow the same path: work hard, get good grades, earn a degree, and get that good job with a bright future. Then, climb the ladder, get the pension and Social Security, and arrive at the oasis of permanent vacation: retirement.

LISA SIDEBAR

Traditional retirement is what I observed as a kid. I watched many people in my community go effortlessly from careers and jobs to retirement. But retirement didn't mean that they quit working: retirees simply found new ways to pursue what they valued.

For example, I had a teacher who could always keep us interested in learning. When it came time to retire, he ended his official teaching career. But he really just moved his classroom to the tennis court, where he taught tennis for many more years.

My dad practiced dentistry for his entire career, and he took great pride in helping his clients. When it was time for him to retire, he jumped directly into volunteer leadership positions in the community.

These two men had something else in common: they always seemed to be smiling. They never lost their passion, and even though they found new paths, they never stopped doing things that they loved. And that has kept them young at heart, vital in their communities, and just plain happy.

Kirk's Story

After graduating from college, Kirk felt the key to success was to get in an industry and stick with it: specialize in that industry and network within it to protect himself in case something happened that threatened his job.

From the beginning, Kirk's goal was to "get the job done, get a bankroll, and retire comfortably" in his early sixties. He knew his job in the paper industry would likely require him to move geographically at least once to grow his career and reach his objectives, and he was willing to be a "corporate gypsy," as he put it. Each time he moved, his company always bought his old home and gave him a down payment on the next; he always made money on the moves.

Kirk lived on his salary; he deferred all of his bonuses to fund the gap between retirement and required minimum distributions from his maximum-funded 401(k). He believed in delayed gratification and in living below his means; he only borrowed to pay for cars and homes. Kirk was proud and happy to save and sacrifice for retirement; he planned to provide not just for himself, but also for his wife and to avoid being a burden for his kids.

His philosophy carried over to the way he managed. For example, when cell phones started coming out, he'd see people talking on them right next to a pay phone on which they could be talking for 25¢ instead of 50¢ per minute. When his salespeople asked for cell phones, Kirk's answer was a roll of quarters!

Kirk had a "fixed plan," a traditional defined-benefit pension based on his last five years' income. Through the years, he received higher salary offers from other companies, but his pension kept him where he was. He retired financially secure at sixty-two, on the very date he had planned on his whole career.

Now that Kirk is in his eighties, his old industry is almost completely gone. Technology has reduced the need for the paper products he used to sell, and the plants he used to support have all closed. Kirk's careful planning—and the era in which he worked—allowed him to achieve the retirement he always wanted.

When I asked him if there were any surprises after retirement, Kirk replied, "How nice it feels to be free."

What allowed this simple and steady view of work and retirement was a US economy that dominated the world, unchallenged by other nations. US companies experienced manageable and predictable rates of change, and while innovation and increased productivity in products and services fueled unprecedented growth, the workplace paradigm remained relatively unchanged for decades.

Throughout these years, each generation enjoyed a better standard of living than the one before it. Homes grew bigger and more lavish. One-car garages gave way to two-, then three-car garages. Postage-stamp lots in the city became a half-acre in the suburbs. The commute was longer, but our automobiles became larger and more comfortable.

Everyone wanted a bigger piece of the pie—which was just fine, because the pie kept getting bigger.

Careers and quality of life evolved and improved. The standard of living was higher, people migrated away from physically demanding jobs, more and more employers provided health care benefits, and that health care improved with each passing year. People were living longer, and better.

What could possibly go wrong?

Ironically, the norm of retiring at sixty-five had unintended consequences. Our collective success began to affect many factors relating to work in America. As our standard of living increased, so did our ambition for the spoils of a wealthy middle class, the quality of our health care, and the rate of innovation.

All of this combined to create a sea change, the consequences of which we are experiencing today. And if you are still thinking about retirement in this traditional sense, that is a problem. Because things have changed . . . and changed significantly.

RETIREMENT NOW AND IN THE FUTURE

There is nothing wrong with change, if it is in the right direction.
—Winston Churchill

Retirement is a very different proposition today. Yet, although some people have a sense of just how different it is, many in their forties, fifties, and sixties are unaware of the breathtaking scope and gravity of those changes.

Today more and more people find themselves working much longer and much harder than they want to, often after being forced into jobs far different from those they had planned. And when they reach the end of their careers, they find that the structures that supported their parents' generation have disappeared or have not kept pace with the cost of living. Nearly every element of traditional retirement has radically changed.

Let's start with the big picture.

The US economy is no longer isolated from the rest of the world and, as a consequence, is subject to far-flung events that influence its stability and strength. Businesses now operate globally, increasing pressures on growth and requiring them to be much more flexible and nimble. Employees, in turn, have the same requirements.

The result is that slow, steady growth is largely a thing of the past for businesses; for employees, the slow, steady climb through the ranks of one company has also passed into the mists of history. Both have been replaced by paths that are increasingly tumultuous, with ups and downs, sharp turns, and—in drastic but not unusual cases—sudden stops.

The financial changes to retirement are no less striking. Social Security is no longer the sure thing that was once believed. The new demographic realities are inescapable: fewer people are paying into the system, while more people are receiving larger benefits for longer periods of time.

Individual pensions are being restructured, and defined-benefit plans have been substantially replaced by defined-contribution plans. As a result, retirement incomes are much less predictable and much more at the mercy of disruptions to the economy. In most parts of the economy, pensions have disappeared completely.

For today's employee, trust in their employer to take care of them throughout their work lives and retirement has eroded dramatically, if not vanished altogether. The one-employer-for-life model is largely a relic of the past.

LISA SIDEBAR

As recently as ten or fifteen years ago, recruiting an individual for a job meant looking for candidates with long tenure. Candidates with ten to twenty years of steady, climbing experience in one company were considered amazing assets. Their dedication reflected loyalty and accomplishment.

Today, employers get concerned when candidates have been at one company for most of their career. They can be viewed as playing it safe, not taking enough chances. Employers wonder, "What's wrong with this person, that they stayed in the same place? Couldn't they get a job elsewhere?"

It is completely possible for staying with one organization to be a strength, but it must be explained and sold, and that's a big shift from past years.

Demographics are also changing the face of retirement. Life expectancy continues to rise in the United States; today people can expect to live eight years longer than they did in 1970. Improvements in immunization, disease control, and overall health care have resulted in many more golden years for today's average retiree, with a subsequent increase in financial requirements.

Because of the turbulent nature of today's work environment, the financial incentives for retirement have reversed. The significant shifts in income during working lives, pension payouts after retirement, and Social Security benefits have resulted in more and more people now wanting—and often needing—to work past age sixty-five.

The combined effect of the new retirement reality is that individuals must fundamentally rethink their approach to retirement.

In years past, retirement planning could be thought of as a landing a helicopter; you arrived at sixty-five and descended straight down to a gentle landing at retirement. Today, we land "through" retirement, not "on" it and retirement planning is more akin to flying an airplane. You, as the pilot, must be more in control much sooner. You have to plan your approach to retirement well before arriving at your chosen retirement age. As you near landing, you must direct your plane through a slow descent and safe landing.

JOHN SIDEBAR

When I begin a discussion of retirement with my clients, I remind them of the assumed life expectancy in my financial plans. For clients who assume retirement at sixty-five, this represents not only the need to fund potentially thirty years of living, but also thirty years of doing something meaningful with their time!

I also advise my clients to "keep the hammer down" by staying current and networking in their field until they retire. Based on their drive and engagement, I anticipate that many of them—to their own astonishment—will reach this point and want to keep working!

Depending on how you think about retirement, this new reality may require a new mindset. Successful retirement now requires thinking differently not just about retirement, but also about your career, your value in the workplace, and your financial planning.

And perhaps most importantly, it requires you to think differently about yourself.

CHARTING YOUR RETIREMENT COURSE

Advice about planning for retirement is, if anything, even harder to offer than general financial planning recommendations. As we mentioned in the previous chapter, the decisions involved are so personal, and the possible situations so numerous and unique, that no system is a sure thing.

But the *Fire Yourself!* process is not about dictating spending—it's about making intentional decisions about how your career and resources support your life and values. We want you to take the controls now and start plotting that long, slow descent through retirement, so that you'll touch down where you want to be, living in a way that represents your priorities, rather than scrambling to make the best of what you've got.

Again, we're assuming that your financial house is in order. And, of course, for personalized planning and expert number crunching, nothing beats the expertise of a financial planner. But before you revisit your 401(k) or make your next appointment at your planner's office, set aside time to discern what you want to achieve specifically in retirement.

You have to take the time to identify where you really want to go. If you formulate a retirement plan before you align your resources with your values, you will end up with a strategy that reflects what you are doing rather than what you want to be doing. Even the most skilled financial planner cannot look into your head and heart and see what matters most to you. Only you can bring that to the table.

Using the information you've gathered so far, take a look at your expectations of retirement in particular.

ZOOM IN ON RETIREMENT

Revisit the timeline you and your spouse or life partner created in the previous chapter. Focus on the years after your projected retirement and detail. Ask yourselves questions such as:

- Will you and your spouse or partner land through retirement together or separately?

- What goals do you hope to achieve together, and individually?
- Do you have any health concerns as it regards you and your spouse, your parents, or your children?
- What legacy would you like to leave your children (if any)?
- Have you made a bucket list? (If you haven't yet, watch the movie The Bucket List!)
- What do you and your spouse like to do together when you're not working?
- How much do you travel now? How much does it cost? How much more or less will you travel once you are retired?
- If time and money were no object, what would you do differently with your day? What would you add to your Bucket List?
- Do you have a mission in mind for your retirement? (i.e., serving your community, doing something for your [future] grandchildren)

Let your imagination run. This is everything you hope to achieve, given all the time and good health in the world.

When you have collected all possible goals on your timeline, prioritize them. Choose your top five or ten retirement must-haves—both together and individually—and sketch out what resources you'll need to achieve them.

ANTICIPATE BEHAVIORAL CHANGES

Revisit the information you gathered about your cash flow. How do you anticipate it changing by the date of your retirement? Which expenses will increase or decrease significantly? How will you prepare for such changes? What other resources will be freed up as your working hours are released back into your control?

Without judgment, and with an open mind, build up a picture of how your overall cash flow will change, and how you will adjust your spending expectations to keep them in line with the values you identified.

RENEW FOCUS ON VALUES

Now you'll need to take a different tack. Instead of firing yourself, stop now and Retire Yourself! Imagine the first day of your well-earned retirement. All of the hours you spend working are now at your disposal. The resources that you have set aside are now available to you again. You have twenty or thirty years—perhaps more—to fill. Where and how do you want to spend them, and what results do you want to achieve? How will you find purpose? What will drive you?

JOHN SIDEBAR

I often remind my clients that stress is underrated! Sometimes the very issues and challenges that create stress in our working years also create the satisfaction of solving problems and achieving goals, not to mention a sense of purpose. Having a mortgage to pay gets you out of bed in the morning!

Look again at your timeline and compare it to your intentional spending plan. As you move into retirement, how will your approach to supporting the things you value change? Are all of your goals achievable in light of your resources? Will you have to make significant and painful changes in your day-to-day spending habits in order to reach those goals, or do you have a comfortable margin that will allow you to achieve those goals or adjust them over time?

Remember that you will be juggling a new resource in retirement: time. Many of our clients reach retirement after dedicating long hours every week to their careers. Without that structure, how will you apply this newly available resource in support of your values? Have a plan.

Remember that retirement doesn't mean abandoning your network. Start looking now for the connections that will support you in reaching your life goals later. Leverage your contacts to find opportunities to give back. Many people choose to share their wisdom by teaching, mentoring, serving on boards, and volunteering. Look back at your career plan and identify goals that excite you and make you feel engaged. Remember: don't be done! Retirement is the perfect time to redirect energies from corporate goals to personal goals of learning and growing, and sharing the fruits of that effort with others.

WRITE IT DOWN

Gather the main points of each section into a summary. What are your top-priority goals for retirement? What changes do you anticipate in resource allocation in order to achieve them, and are you on track to have those resources available? How will your use of those resources support your values as you enter your golden years?

Bring a copy of this summary to your financial planning meetings, or file it with your retirement documents. Revisit it (and the entire exercise, if need be) each year, revising your goals as your career matures and your values evolve. Everything changes: revisit your strategy regularly to keep it in sync with your lived experience. If you make time to stay in touch with your values, you'll be better able to keep them in view through any times of upheaval, and they'll be much closer when you finally make that retirement landing.

CHAPTER 10

IN CLOSING

I've learned that no matter what happens, or
how bad it seems today, life does go on, and
it will be better tomorrow.

—*Maya Angelou*

We hope you have found this book to be helpful—and even inspirational—for the future of your career.

Though the times we live in are chaotic, complex, and ever-changing, they are also times of tremendous possibilities. We all face challenges and opportunities, and how we choose to face them will determine our personal success.

No one can predict what is coming next. Whether you stay in your role for the next twenty years or suddenly realize it's time for a change, make it your choice! Our aim has been to convince you that a career driven by purpose, passion, and choice is much more fulfilling, rewarding, and financially sound.

You have the power to create the future you want. Once you have decided to own that power, grab the reins, and put it forth in the world, you are on your way. The path won't be easy, but it will be yours. When you know where you want to go, take action, and ask for help, people will appear to support you with your new endeavor. Don't wait! Articulate what you want and go after it!

There will be unexpected twists and turns. But as you go forward, we know you'll discover strengths, skills, and possibilities you could never have imagined.

It has been said that the tragedy of life is not that we are going to die; it's that we may die before ever having truly lived. Our goal has been to help you find the courage and clarity to do just that: truly live the life you want—a life of value, joy, and fulfillment.

Nothing is going to stay the same; everything is always about to change. This simply means the possibilities for your happiness are endless.

So we'll remind you of the core message of *Fire Yourself!*

Don't be done.

Don't be done figuring out where you are. Don't be done figuring out where you want to go. Don't be done figuring out how to get there.

Don't be done learning. Don't be done growing. Don't be done with your life's work.

Plan to revisit this process on a regular basis as you grow and learn. By now you should be certain that change is inevitable, and as you weather those unavoidable changes to the plan—good or bad—you can return to these exercises in order to modify your strategy and stay focused on your end goals. Life may create obstacles in your path, but if you stay focused on where you want to go, you will be well prepared to forge a new path to your goal.

There are no shortcuts to career and retirement success. It might seem like it, but they actually take longer—if they work at all. That's why it's vital to seize control of your career, recognize the signs of change, and know when it's time to move forward.

We hope you enjoy the rewards of taking charge of your career and the journey of finding that happiness. And when you do, we want to hear from you! Visit our website at FireYourselfNow. com and follow us on Twitter at @FireYourselfNow.

ABOUT THE AUTHORS

John Rusciano joined Northwestern Mutual after more than a decade as an executive in telecommunications and real estate investment. As a Wealth Management Advisor, he helps clients to align their resources and career strategies with their highest held values, driving thoughtful and intentional financial planning decisions. John is a volunteer to the Minnesota Fire Service Foundation, is a NOAA Skywarn volunteer and Extra Class amateur radio operator. John lives in Minnetonka, Minnesota, with his wife, COO, and business partner, Koren, and has three grown children, Jessica, Julia, and Mark. John can be reached at www.johnrusciano.com.

Lisa Brezonik has more than twenty years of experience in leading and coaching individuals maneuvering change and growth. After holding HR leadership roles at several national and international companies, she founded an executive coaching and organizational consulting firm that created solutions for both individual and organizational growth. Lisa is currently Chief Talent Officer at Salo, LLC, a consulting firm that offers solutions for finance, accounting, and HR. Lisa serves on the board of the Ann Bancroft Foundation. She lives in Minneapolis, Minnesota, with her husband, Nick, and her children Sarah, Joe, Billy and Niko.

Made in the USA
San Bernardino, CA
19 September 2016